The
100 Best
Businesses
to Start When You
Don't Want to
Work Hard
Anymore

The
100 Best
Businesses
to Start When You
Don't Want to
Work Hard
Anymore

CAREER
PRESS

Franklin Lakes, NJ

THE 100 BEST BUSINESSES TO START WHEN YOU
DON'T WANT TO WORK HARD ANYMORE
EDITED BY CLAYTON W. LEADBETTER
TYPESET BY STACEY A. FARKAS
Cover design by Foster & Foster, Inc.
Printed in the U.S.A. by Book-mart Press

To order this title, please call toll-free 1-800-CAREER-1 (NJ and Canada: 201-848-0310) to order using VISA or MasterCard, or for further information on books from Career Press.

The Career Press, Inc., 3 Tice Road, PO Box 687,
Franklin Lakes, NJ 07417
www.careerpress.com

Library of Congress Cataloging-in-Publication Data

Rogak, Lisa, 1962-
    The 100 best businesses to start when you don't want to work hard anymore / by Lisa Rogak.
        p. cm.
    Includes index.
    ISBN 1-56414-736-3 (paper)
    1. New business enterprises. 2. Small business—Management. 3. Self-employed. 4.
Career changes. 5. Retirees—Employment. I. Title: One hundred best businesses to start when you don't want to work hard anymore. II. Title: Best businesses to start when you don't want to work hard anymore. III. Title.

    HD62.5.R629 2004
    658.1'141--dc22

                                                    2004045853

Dedication

For Black Kitty, Demon Kitty, and Stinky —

great role models to have if you

don't want to work hard anymore.

Contents

Part II: Entrepreneurship 101, 177

Introduction

Take this job and shove it, indeed.

Some days, Johnny Paycheck just had it nailed.

In the mundane world of making a living, we all have those days when the last thing we want is to be on the clock, sweating away for somebody else. But some people feel like this for months, possibly years—maybe even you. In this case, it's not your boss, coworkers, or the job itself that you're not crazy about; it's the work. In other words, you don't feel like spending eight or more hours a day at something that feels like, well, *work*.

Whenever you read news stories about people who run their own businesses and love what they do, it just rubs it in more. "It doesn't seem like work," these entrepreneurs all but gush, "I'm getting paid to play all day."

"Sign me up," you say. But in the next breath, you dismiss the thought as a ludicrous idea. "I don't have any special talent—no one would pay me to play."

Think again. You don't have to be a burned-out 40-something to hate to work; people just out of college may feel this way with their first jobs. Retirees especially may agree, given the decades they spent toiling at a hated job as well as the lowered energy level that commonly arrives with age.

It is possible for you to launch a business that's perfect for you, in which every minute you spend will seem like anything but work.

But what will you do? Lacking a trust fund or a rich spouse, how will you leave behind your bread-and-butter job for the insecurity of no paycheck and running your own show?

The answer is simple: If your expectations are halfway realistic, and if you love what you do, it's likely that everything will fall into place. Of course, you may have to start by taking baby steps at first, starting your business part-time. Then again, that's how many entrepreneurs start out.

Some of the businesses in this book are service-oriented, such as pet-sitting and becoming a massage therapist, while in others you'd be creating a product. Still others are retail-oriented, including selling used books and baking customized cakes for weddings and other special occasions. You may want to turn a beloved, lifelong hobby into a business, or you may want to start a business based on a total fantasy, such as running a bed-and-breakfast.

In any case, once you start one of these don't-want-to-work businesses, I can say one thing: You probably won't get rich. But then, if you're reading this book, that doesn't much matter, does it?

What makes a business perfect if you don't want to work hard anymore? As you page through the book and the list of businesses, there are undoubtedly a few that don't strike you as "easy" businesses to start. Keep in mind, someone's definition of "hard" and "easy" businesses may be a 180-degree turn away from yours. For instance, most people, would consider masonry a business where hard work is the rule. However, someone who loves to be physical all day while executing projects with a surgeon's skill would be pretty happy.

Another consideration in selecting a business is, of course, the investment required. There are many variables, according to whether you already own some of the tools necessary for a particular business, such as for furniture making, or even the building, as in the case of a bed-and-breakfast. Throughout the text, I provide investment levels using the terms *high*, *medium*, and *low*. Admittedly, because my sensibilities tend toward the frugal Yankee sort—I am one by nature, if not by birth—some readers may find my estimates on the low side. As well, it can strongly depend on the area of the country in which you choose to do business. But roughly, the following are the ranges used:

> Low: $0-10,000
> Medium: $10,000-25,000
> High: $25,000 or more

In choosing to start your own business, there are several criteria, any number of which may apply in your case:

▶   The business you choose is 100 percent pure fun.

- The business may be a thinly-disguised version of your previous job, but in its entrepreneurial incarnation, the hourly rate means you can work only a fraction of the time.
- The business is an extension of a favorite hobby, and your financial future will not ride on the revenue it generates.
- The business is a dream come true, something you've always yearned to do.

Regardless of your responses to these points, what matters is that you love what you do. Because once you love what you do, then even the routine tasks necessary to run any business won't seem like work.

Part I:
The Businesses

1. Adventure Travel Outfitting

 Description of the business: A company where guides lead vacationers and tourists on trips in the wilderness.

 Why it's a good business to start if you don't want to work hard anymore: People are becoming more interested in going on challenging nature trips, but many feel more comfortable relying on an experienced guide who will show them the ropes. It's a good business because you can spend most of your time traveling the world.

 Skills necessary: Being a people person helps, and you'll need the ability to negotiate with suppliers and other businesses to get the materials and accommodations you'll need to make your customers happy.

Investment required: Medium.

? **For more information:** Adventure Travel Society, 4555 Southlake Parkway, Birmingham, AL 35244; 866-233-2053; *www.adventuretravel.com*

If you've always loved to be active in the outdoors—whether canoeing, hiking, horseback riding, or mountain climbing—and your idea of paradise is getting paid to do it, then you should think about starting a business that lets you do just that. If you want to start a business as an adventure travel outfitter, you'll have to help people who have less experience in the wild than you do, as well as market your services to them in the first place, but for people who would rather die than spend their days sitting behind a desk, it's an ideal choice.

Today many people like to experience some degree of adventure when they go on vacation; the flip side is that they want to feel safe while doing it. That's where you, as an adventure travel outfitter, will fit right in. Basically, you'll serve as a tour guide for your clients, mapping out a satisfying itinerary, arranging for nightly accommodations, knowing in advance where to find a decent lunch along your route, and teaching your charges the basics. However, you'll discover that you'll spend more time planning the trip than being on the road. In fact, many outfitters get so busy that they rarely go out on trips, after the first year or two they're in business, and have to rely instead on hired guides to lead the groups.

Adventure travel is popular these days, and you'll face a good deal of competition, especially as you strive to establish yourself. But if you can set your business apart in some way, creating a niche market—maybe you'll focus on offering dude ranch weekends or specialize in helping women in their 40s learn how to hike and camp out—your chances for success improve greatly. Just be aware that, in this business, success means you'll probably have to stay home and run the show.

2. Alternative Medical Consulting

 Description of the business: A medical practitioner advises clients and physicians on the best kinds of alternative medical methods for a given illness or condition.

 Why it's a good business to start if you don't want to work hard anymore: More people—patients and physicians—are turning to alternative medical practices to supplement the traditional care they receive. You can use previous medical skills in a totally different way.

 Skills necessary: A background in traditional medicine will give you credibility; you'll need both clinical and research experience in a variety of alternative medical practices as well.

 Investment required: Medium.

 For more information: Complementary Alternative Medical Association, PO Box 373478, Decatur, GA 30037; 404-284-7592; *www.camaweb.org*

Alternative medicine is hot and getting hotter all the time. It's been widely reported that one out of four American adults have visited at least one alternative medical practitioner in the last year, in addition to seeing a traditional physician. Now that many health insurance plans are starting to cover everything from acupuncture to Ayurvedic medicine, patients and physicians who may have become disenchanted with traditional medicine are beginning to explore the variety of alternative practices to help ease their condition. However, sifting through the numerous methods that exist—as well as locating qualified practitioners—can consume exorbitant amounts of time, which few patients and physicians have.

That's where alternative medicine consultants come in. Well-versed in the protocol of traditional medicine and knowledgeable about where to find the necessary information about alternative medical practices to pass along to physicians and patients, an alternative medicine consultant serves as a kind of clearinghouse for patients and their physicians, pointing doctors in the right direction and advising patients on the effects that different therapies will have on a particular condition.

An alternative medical consultant can advise patients and physicians and provide them with written documents and studies, counseling both individually or collectively. She can also recommend certain therapies and point out the pros and cons of others. Diplomacy helps because in the past they have eschewed working together. They are learning to work cooperatively, however; alternative medicine and traditional medicine are both here to stay. A specialized consultant can help both to work side by side for a common good: the well-being of the patient.

3. Antiques Business

 Description of the business: A venture that involves the buying and selling of antiques and collectibles, either in a rented booth in an antiques mall, in your own shop, at shows, over the Internet, or any combination of these.

 Why it's a good business to start if you don't want to work hard anymore: As the frenzy over Beanie Babies shows, many people are natural-born collectors who gather up antiques and collectibles as a time-consuming and obsessive hobby.

 Skills necessary: An eye for what is valuable and in demand and the knowledge of quality items.

 Investment required: Low.

 For more information: *How to Start a Home-Based Antiques Business,* by Jacquelyn Peake (Globe Pequot Press, 2000).

Many antiques entrepreneurs will cheerfully admit that they got into the antiques business because they had accumulated too much stuff and had to get rid of some, thus allowing them to go out and buy more, because the hunt is the addictive part of collecting.

But not all of these people are able to make a go of their addictions as a business; indeed, for some, it's not the point. The great thing about running an antiques business is that it can be successful in many different forms and on many different levels. You can cut back at certain times of the year and go full steam ahead when people are in a buying mood. Plus, the Internet has made the art of making money by selling antiques and collectibles into a much more viable venture simply because you can buy from and sell to another person regardless of where they live.

Of course, purchasing an item before you can handle it has its downsides, but on the whole, the end result is that the entire world is your market.

Besides the type of antiques businesses already described, an antiques business owner can also dabble in the fields of appraising, restoration and repair, and auctioneering. These fields will allow you to continue to make money from your love of antiques even during a lull in the market for your particular specialty.

Furthermore, because more people are competing for a steadily dwindling number of quality antiques in a businesses where the stakes and the risks can be quite steep, experts advise that the most important way to minimize your risk in the antiques business is to have an eye for what sells within your chosen field. In other words, specialize.

4. Appliance Repair

 Description of the business: A service where a person skilled in diagnosing and fixing household appliances travels to local households to make the necessary repairs.

 Why it's a good business to start if you don't want to work hard anymore: As appliances get more computerized in nature, a repair job frequently isn't the quick fix it was a decade earlier. Skilled help is often needed, and the hourly rate can be significant.

 Skills necessary: You'll need at least one year of experience working as an apprentice to an appliance repairman, or six month of vocational school, and the technical proficiency in order to succeed.

 Investment required: Medium.

 For more information: Contact local vocational and technical schools.

If you decide that an appliance repair business is for you, you'll probably always have more work than you can handle repairing dryers, refrigerators, stoves, and dishwashers.

The majority of appliance repairmen work by themselves, and are able to take on six or seven jobs in one day, depending upon the time necessary to travel from one job to the next. The average job is about an hour long. Experienced repairmen report that the biggest downside to the job is that customers are not always here when they arrive.

Marketing is easy. It's primarily done through word of mouth, although a small newspaper ad will usually be enough to start the phone ringing when you first "hang out your shingle." Perhaps the best way to get a steady flow of work is to arrange to take on repair referrals from a local appliance store, especially if their own staff of repair workers tend to be overburdened with work. Warranty work contracted out by the manufacturer of an appliance will also account for some of a repairman's workload.

As an appliance repairperson, you will need to occasionally close down shop to attend training sessions about new appliances and technologies. These regular classes are typically run by the appliance manufacturers, such as General Electric and Maytag. As appliances continue to get more technical and integrate new computer software and hardware into their operating systems, it's necessary for the people who repair them to keep current.

5. Automobile Detailing

 Description of the business: A service that cleans a client's car to perfection, inside and out, either at their own location or at the customer's home or office.

 Why it's a good business to start if you don't want to work hard anymore: People are spending more money on their cars, and they have less time to perform routine maintenance on and clean their vehicles. You can work as much or as little as you want, and you can go directly to customers or have them come to you.

 Skills necessary: It helps if you're a perfectionist and love cars.

 Investment required: Medium.

 For more information: Rightlook.com, 7616 Miramar Road, Suite 5300, San Diego, CA 92126; 800-883-3446; *www.rightlook.com*

America has always been chock-full of car lovers, and although many people love to lavish the care and attention on their vehicles necessary to make them sparkle and shine, few have the time for it.

Enter the relatively new field of automobile detailing, where a stickler for a clean car goes through a customer's car with a fine-tooth comb, cleaning, vacuuming, washing, and waxing a vehicle—a process that can take an entire day or more, depending upon the car and the owner. Car detailing is a great business for a vicarious car lover, who drools upon spotting an ultra-expensive and luxurious Jaguar or Bentley, but who might not be able to afford such a vehicle in this lifetime.

The great thing about running a car-detailing business is that it actually costs less to start up if you operate primarily as a mobile business (that is, you go to your customers and work on their vehicles on their premises). In this case, you'll save on the cost of equipping a garage to work in, although in mobile work it may sometimes be inconvenient to find a reliable water source and to work outdoors in inclement weather.

Anyplace there's a population of people with expensive cars and not enough time to care for them is an area where a car detailing business will thrive. The good news is that your work is your best calling card; savvy car detailers make up little stickers or customized license plate holders for their clients that read "This car detailed by _____."

6. Bakery

 Description of the business: A business that provides freshly baked breads, cookies, cakes, pastries, and light meals to consumers and/or wholesale accounts.

 Why it's a good business to start if you don't want to work hard anymore: People are catching quick meals on the run, which sometimes consist of a pastry and coffee. Bakeries are well equipped to help meet this need.

 Skills necessary: You'll need to have basic baking skills, or if you're going for the upscale market, a culinary arts education will go a long way.

 Investment required: Medium.

 For more information: Retailer's Bakery Association, 14239 Park Center Drive, Laurel, MD 20707; 301-725-2149; *www.rbanet.com*

In the 21st century, anything that is hand-crafted and of high quality will be in much demand. That goes as much for baked goods as it does for handmade furniture and homes.

Opening a bakery is a smart move because people are grabbing meals on the run and buying more desserts and other baked goods to take home; they just don't have enough time. The good news is that many new and established bakeries are serving two separate markets in one space: the walk-in consumer market, as well as the wholesale market, selling to restaurants, supermarkets, cafés, and other establishments that serve food. Frequently, in the beginning, it's necessary for a bakery to have both markets in order to pay the bills while staying afloat.

Before you launch your research into starting a bakery, however, you'll need to possess a love for long hours that frequently start in the middle of the night, or you'll need to find employees who don't mind starting their workday when it's dark out. Because a bakery is a labor-intensive business, perhaps more so than the other enterprises described in this book, you may need to spend more of your time dealing with personnel issues than entrepreneurs in other businesses. However, if you love to cook and create baked goods from scratch and the aroma and the smiles on your customers' faces are more than enough to sustain you, then starting a bakery may be just the thing for you.

7. Bed-and-Breakfast

 Description of the business: A private house with a number of guest rooms that are rented out overnight or longer to guests. Breakfast is served each morning.

 Why it's a good business to start if you don't want to work hard anymore: Many travelers prefer to stay in 'homelike, intimate places where they know the owners and can mingle with other guests. You can live where you work and get paid to take care of people on vacation.

 Skills necessary: You must be a people person.

 Investment required: Medium.

For more information: Professional Association of Innkeepers International, PO Box 90710, Santa Barbara, CA 93190; 805-569-1853; *www.paii.org*

Everyone who has ever stayed at a bed-and-breakfast usually ends up telling the owners that they'd like to trade places. What most people don't realize is that running a

successful B and B takes more than it seems on the surface. Besides having a lot of energy and a background in cooking and entertaining, a B and B host also has to like living in a state of near-crisis and operating on a shoestring most of the time. If all these things apply, then a B and B is the perfect business for you.

There is more to running a B and B than meets the eye. You have to make sure the house meets state safety codes, so you may need to install a hardwired smoke and fire alarm system, for example, if one does not already exist. Marketing is usually a sore spot with B and B keepers, but the process can be streamlined by joining the local Chamber of Commerce and the local association of resort owners and tourism boards. Advertising is key, as visibility in guidebooks and other travel publications will help to pull in guests. Your hospitality will turn visitors into repeat guests—the lifeblood of success in the industry.

Most B and Bs don't have the number of rooms of their larger cousin, the full-fledged inn, and lack the revenue stream to support employees. So bear in mind that as a B and B host, most of the work will be up to you. From cleaning toilets to chopping vegetables, you should be prepared to do it all.

Running a B and B is a great business if you're a homebody but still want to see the world; in a B and B, the world will come to see you, and you can develop some close-knit friendships with people from all over the world. If you're not afraid of long hours and love to show off your neck of the woods to travelers, then a B and B would be a good business for you.

8. Bookkeeping

 Description of the business: A venture that helps keep the financial records for other businesses.

 Why it's a good business to start if you don't want to work hard anymore: As more people start their own businesses, they'll want to outsource as many tasks as possible; bookkeeping is the most popular to farm out. Sophisticated software programs make an independent bookkeeping service a good candidate for a high hourly rate.

 Skills necessary: You'll need a background in or a passion for accounting and a familiarity with spreadsheets and budgets.

 Investment required: Low.

? **For more information:** *Bookkeeping and Tax Preparation: Start and Build a Prosperous Bookkeeping, Tax, and Financial Services Business,* by Gordon P. Lewis (Acton Circle Publishing Company, 1996).

Most people start their own businesses because they have a passion for the product or service they're providing, not for maintaining the financial records necessary to keep a business up and running. However, if you have a passion for numbers, and if you decide to start your own bookkeeping business, you'll find a significant number of small business owners eager to give you the opportunity to manage their books for them.

Whether you decide to focus on one-person businesses or larger enterprises, all you really need is an aptitude for numbers and a powerful accounting software program. You may want to specialize in a particular industry—such as restaurants or computer consultants—where keeping accurate records and generating timely

accounts payable and receivable is vital to the short- and long-term health of the business. For example, if a restaurant doesn't pay its suppliers on time on a weekly basis, it might not have enough beer or meat for the next week. Specializing in one industry also makes it easier for you, because the number of categories in a spreadsheet will remain relatively consistent throughout your work.

If you're the type of person who loves to work with numbers all day long and you want to serve as a vitally important arm of a business—while being in control of your own business—then starting a bookkeeping business may be a good bet for you.

9. Business Plan Writing

 Description of the business: Researching and writing business plans for new and experienced entrepreneurs.

 Why it's a good business to start if you don't want to work hard anymore: Many people want to start their own businesses, and they know they need a business plan, but most won't have a clue about what makes one business plan more successful than another. They'll need to turn to an expert for advice, and they're willing to pay good money for a plan that will help them secure financing.

 Skills necessary: Obviously, the ability to write a persuasive business plan is key, along with a talent for quickly learning the quirks of an industry in order to incorporate relevant facts into a plan.

 Investment required: Low.

 For more information: *The Business Planning Guide: Creating a Plan for Success in Your Own Business (9th Edition)*, by David H. Bangs (Upstart Publishing, 2002).

Despite the proliferation of books, manuals, and software packages that promise their users will be able to write a complete business plan in an evening, the truth is that, because every startup is unique, new entrepreneurs need to customize their business plans according to the constraints of a particular industry while also skewing it towards the investors and employees who will read the plan.

If you have experience writing business plans that have achieved their forecasts and their goals—whether it's attracting capital or providing a timeline to guide the owner through a business's first year—you'll likely do well as a business plan writer. Aspiring entrepreneurs will look to you for help and advice, while experienced business owners who don't have the time to write a plan will consult with you to take the hard facts of their business, as well as the financial figures, and assemble the information into a coherent business plan.

As entrepreneurs at all levels of experience and in all industries continue to look for whatever will give them the edge over their competitors and impress investors, they know that a well-written business plan that covers all aspects of their venture is one of the best keys to success down the road. Help them to achieve this end, and you'll never need to write a business plan for your own enterprise again.

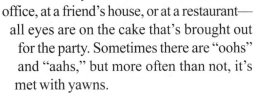

10. Cake Decorating

 Description of the business: An individual makes custom decorated cakes for special occasions that are sold through stores or by word of mouth.

 Why it's a good business to start if you don't want to work hard anymore: Customized home-baked cakes are going to be more in demand as people have less time for baking and don't want to settle for the cookie-cutter cakes available in supermarket bakery sections.

 Skills necessary: You should get some training by taking a cake-decorating class, sometimes available through a local adult school, or by apprenticing with a more experienced cake decorator.

 Investment required: Low.

 For more information: Wilton Industries, 2240 West 75th Street, Woodridge, IL 60517; 630-963-1818; *www.wilton.com*

Whenever someone celebrates a birthday—whether it's at home, at the office, at a friend's house, or at a restaurant—all eyes are on the cake that's brought out for the party. Sometimes there are "oohs" and "aahs," but more often than not, it's met with yawns.

Despite America's obsession with weight loss and low-carb and low-fat foods, a birthday or other special event is still an effortless excuse to celebrate with a cake. Increasingly, people are looking for something a bit different—more elegant or even more outrageous—to make that cake stand out.

Starting a cake baking and decorating business is a can't-lose situation everywhere, even the most rural areas, because people always need a cake and they're willing to pay a little extra for a personal touch and service. In summertime, cake entrepreneurs usually find their workload doubled because people don't want to be bothered with a hot oven.

To get started as an independent cake baker, you can put an ad in the paper, display some cakes at a local convenience store (especially if your area lacks a regular bakery), or work with bridal consultants and shops to display a card listing your services. Some cake bakers start by offering their services as backup for more established cake decorators in the area, especially during the particularly busy months of May and June. One cake decorator with years of experience says she's always looking for someone to whom she can pass along extra work.

As for training, a cake-decorating course helps, along with lots of practice. But even if you start with the simplest of cake designs, and provide a cake that's rich and delicious, word will quickly get around.

11. Carpentry

 Description of the business: A business where a skilled craftsman works with wood to build houses, commercial structures, and building additions, and may work on industrial projects such as constructing the initial framework for roads and bridges.

 Why it's a good business to start if you don't want to work hard anymore: There are always opportunities for skilled carpenters due to turnover and a low influx of new carpenters entering the field. The hourly rate tends to be high and seasonal, so you can take off half the year if you'd like in many cases.

 Skills necessary: You should be detail-oriented and familiar with different kinds of wood. An eye for accuracy and the ability to read blueprints are also important.

 Investment required: Low.

For more information: Associated Builders and Contractors, 4250 North Fairfax Drive, Arlington, VA 22203; 703-812-2000; *www.abc.org*

Most of the carpenters who are working full-time today have been putting pieces of wood together since they were small. For many, this form of life experience serves as their apprenticeship into becoming a carpenter, although some opt for a formal apprenticeship program through a local union or with an established carpentry firm.

Self-employed carpenters can usually call their own shots, either by specializing in a particular field—such as house framing or home improvements—or by choosing to generalize. The lack of skilled workers and the apparently insatiable desire to put up new buildings and work on old ones means that, in many areas of the country, homeowners must wait a year or longer for a skilled carpenter to fit their job into his schedule.

Obviously, anyone who can hold a hammer can call himself a carpenter, but your rates and reputation will undoubtedly increase with the right credentials and a strong track record. Carpentry is physically demanding, and smart entrepreneurs will realize that a solid 20 years in the business is good. Later, when the body starts to rebel against the difficult labor and years of bending and stooping, it's easy to scale back and either supervise other carpenters or migrate to less strenuous fields, such as furniture making and repair.

12. Children's Party Planning

 Description of the business: A venture that takes charge of all of the behind-the-scenes work of planning a party for a child's birthday or other occasion.

 Why it's a good business to start if you don't want to work hard anymore: Especially with both parents working full-time jobs outside the house, few want to spend their leisure time blowing up balloons and making party favors—and cleaning up afterwards.

 Skills necessary: You'll need to be organized and to be able to plan all of the tasks and steps necessary to bring a successful party into the world.

 Investment required: Low.

 For more information: *Getting Started in Event/Party Planning,* Teleseminar Program presented by Phyllis Cambria and Patty Sachs; *www.partyplansplus.com/teleseminarpage.html.*

If you're happiest when planning a party for a family member or even a coworker and you live in an area where parents spend lots of money on their kids, you should think about starting a business where you can spend your time planning parties for kids.

Of course, today's kids are pretty demanding, and a stint at the bowling alley or a visit to Chuck E. Cheese's is probably not going to cut it. So it's important to have a good idea of what boys and girls in different age groups enjoy in order to help foster a successful party and therefore spread your reputation.

As a party planner, you'll design and send out the invitations, locate a suitable venue for the event, purchase or create appropriate favors, prepare the food and drink—or hire a caterer—and clean up afterwards. This way, of course, the parents can spend time with the children during the parties instead of rushing around making sure everything is on schedule. This is the best way to win over the hearts of *other* parents, so you can end up planning their children's parties as well.

Party planners usually charge a fee per child and then charge the cost of food, favors, room rental, and other incidentals directly to the parents. But regardless of the cost, more and more harried parents are going to be willing to hand over the reins to an outside business so they can relax at their children's parties and not sweat the details.

13. Children's Transportation

 Description of the business: Provide door-to-door transportation for children for after school lessons, sports activities, and visits to friends' houses.

 Why it's a good business to start if you don't want to work hard anymore: Parents are working longer hours and are unable to transport their children to frequently packed after-school schedules. A taxi service for kids will be in demand in upper middle-class suburbs where both parents tend to work.

 Skills necessary: A clean driving record and a good rapport with kids—as well as a good dose of patience—are vital.

 Investment required: Medium.

 For more information: *Careers for Kids at Heart and Others Who Adore Children,* by Marjorie Eberts (McGraw-Hill, 1999).

Kids today have schedules packed just as tightly as their parents. Until the advent of specialized taxi services for kids, many children had to pass up favorite activities or events because they lacked a reliable form of transportation.

This is why taxi services for kids are now an accepted part of the landscape in many suburban towns where both parents work and kids are scheduled to the hilt. Even if a taxi service already exists in your area,

chances are that the demand is so strong for regular after school transportation for kids that you should have no problem rustling up a list of clients who will need your services on a regular basis, maybe even every day during the week.

The good news is that a children's transportation service can easily be run on a part-time basis because most of your "deliveries" will be taking place after school and possibly even on weekends, though a few exceptions can occur when doctor's appointments take place during school hours or even before school in areas where there's no regular school or city bus service. You should invest in the largest van you can get (some of the full-size vans can carry up to 12 people) and take the time to map out the most efficient routes each day given your charges' schedules and locations. If you've driven a school bus in the past—and liked it—running your own taxi service for kids will be a piece of cake.

14. Classic Car Sales

 Description of the business: A business that buys and sells classic and antique cars. Restoration and repair services may also be offered.

 Why it's a good business to start if you don't want to work hard anymore: We are a nostalgic people. As Americans grow older, have more money to play with, and look back fondly on the toys of their youth, more will choose to purchase the same model of car they had as a young adult.

 Skills necessary: You need to be able to purchase a car as cheaply as possible, fix it up as best you can, if necessary, and find buyers, some of whom may live clear across the country.

 Investment required: Medium.

 For more information: *Hemmings Motor News,* PO Box 100, Bennington, VT 05201; 800-227-4373; *www.hemmings.com*

In our neck of the woods, you know it's spring when the old cars come out of hiding; some owners can't even wait until the last of the snow has disappeared.

Americans love their cars, whether they're brand-new or 40 (or more) years old. Among the millions of people who dream of turning their hobby into a thriving business, we'd venture to say that old car nuts are probably the ones who fantasize about it the most, probably because they already

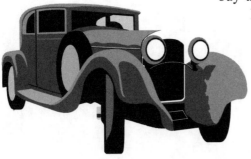

buy and sell cars and, therefore, have a taste of what it could be like if the volume were to be increased to a full-time basis.

State legislation governs the degree to which you can achieve this volume, however. In New Hampshire, for instance, the state allows private citizens to buy and sell up to five cars each year before they start to get suspicious, while in neighboring Vermont, residents can buy and sell as many cars as they want. If you plan to specialize in fixing up one car at a time and restoring it to show condition before reselling it to a deep-pocketed collector, you probably wouldn't have the time to work on more than five cars a year if you run a one-person shop.

Regardless of the state you live in, the key to success in classic car sales is to buy them as cheaply as possible, fix and clean them up so they appeal to buyers, and then use the profits to buy another. Some classic car nuts specialize in a particular model while others become generalists. If you have an eye for collectible models, you might not even have to spend any time fixing them up if you can buy them cheaply enough before reselling it to someone who's been looking for that exact car to restore as a hobby.

15. Cleaning Service

 Description of the business: A company that cleans houses, apartments, and offices on an ongoing or one-time basis.

 Why it's a good business to start if you don't want to work hard anymore: As the leisure time of Americans continues to decrease while their disposable income increases, people are more willing to hire somebody else to do the work they don't want to do. Housecleaning is at the top of the list, and a high hourly rate is the rule for this business.

 Skills necessary: You should like to do physical work and be able to deal with people who may be picky about the cleanliness of their homes.

 Investment required: Low.

? **For more information:** *Start & Run a Home Cleaning Business,* by Susan Bewsey (Self-Counsel Press, 2003).

Some business experts believe that a home- and office-cleaning business is the fastest-growing service industry of the next 10 years and that there will be no letup in sight. If you're thinking about starting a cleaning service, you can expect that, once you hang up a simple card on the bulletin board at the supermarket offering your services, your phone will start to ring off the hook, and you'll probably be fully booked with more work than you can handle in just a few weeks.

Most house cleaners like to clean an entire house instead of taking care of just a few rooms, because when you count the travel time between jobs, your hourly rate quickly diminishes. You can charge by the hour or by the job, but if you're a particularly quick worker, you'll probably make more when you can charge by the job.

Once you witness the demand for cleaning services in your area, you might want to take on an employee or two in order to maximize your revenue. However, you should be aware that the biggest challenges that cleaning services face, no matter where they're located or what the economy is doing, are finding good employees and keeping them motivated. Some business owners have learned, for example, to target people who already have a full-time job and are looking for a sideline to augment their income.

In any case, running a cleaning service means you'll never lack for work.

16. Computer Consulting

 Description of the business: A business that helps individuals and other businesses use their computer systems more efficiently. Services may include support and training, upgrading, and troubleshooting.

 Why it's a good business to start if you don't want to work hard anymore: As computers will undoubtedly become more entrenched in the everyday lives of most Americans, the need for skilled consultants available for a variety of concerns will continue to increase.

 Skills necessary: Computer proficiency is a given, as is logical thinking and the ability to communicate with clients in terms and language they can understand.

 Investment required: Low.

 For more information: Independent Computer Consultants Association, 11131 South Towne Square, St. Louis, MO 63123; 800-774-4222; *www.icca.org*

Computers are here to stay. Ironically, as people find them simpler to use, the mechanics behind most computer operations—hardware and software—have become more complex and difficult for average users to understand, let alone to repair and customize.

Enter the computer consultant, who begins a relationship with a client by asking about the purpose for the computer, and then retrofitting a computer system with hardware and software that allows the client to get his work done without worrying about the mechanics. Though many consultants work with businesses and individuals on a one-time basis, for which they are paid an hourly wage, others prefer to negotiate a monthly retainer with a client, which makes sense—particularly in the case of a system that requires ongoing tweaking and customization as new needs arise.

Depending upon your background and desire, if you decide to open up shop as a computer consultant, you can opt to specialize in a particular industry (catering specifically to lawyers or physicians, for instance), field (such as Internet connectivity or maintaining a company-wide network), or business size (from corporations to one-person offices). There has long been a shortage of skilled computer consultants in all areas. If you know your stuff, it's likely that you'll be able to write your own ticket as a computer consultant for years to come.

17. Computer Network Administration

Description of the business: A business that is responsible for designing and maintaining the network of computers a company's employees rely on.

Why it's a good business to start if you don't want to work hard anymore: Computer networks are more the rule than the exception at offices these days, allowing employees to share software, hardware, and files. However, many offices still do not have a network set up, and those that do need a computer expert to help maintain and troubleshoot the system.

Skills necessary: You'll need to be comfortable working with computers and networks and be able to clearly communicate instructions and details to people who may not be computer savvy.

Investment required: Medium.

For more information: Network Professional Association, 17 South High Street, Suite 200, Columbus, OH, 43215; 888-672-6720; *www.npa.org*

Studies on technical jobs and careers frequently state that hundreds of thousands of computer-related jobs go unfilled because of a lack of skilled professionals. This statistic applies more often to network specialists, who

are entrusted with designing a system appropriate for an office and providing technical support to employees when the system goes down, sometimes a frequent occurrence.

While many companies would love to have a full-time network specialist, they are facing one of two dilemmas: They may not be able to afford a staff consultant, or they may not be able to find one. That's why an outside networking service could be one of the most popular and successful high-tech businesses for the future. In fact, one aspect of a networking business could feasibly consist of serving consumers who are starting to set up a network of computers, printers, and software in their own homes and who need guidance in the process, as well as someone to call with questions and for advice.

The downside to opening a network consulting business is that you may have more work than you can handle within days of opening up shop. In this case, you can limit the number of clients you serve or hire people to help you. However, you may need to get inventive about who you hire and where you find them, because the downside of this hot technical employment market will have come full circle.

18. Computer Repair

 Description of the business: A business that specializes in fixing the computers of individuals and businesspeople, by making house calls, opening a storefront, or providing a diagnosis and solution over the phone or e-mail.

 Why it's a good business to start if you don't want to work hard anymore: As computers get more complicated and high-powered, fewer people will possess the skills to repair them when something goes wrong. If you can keep up with the latest in hardware and software, you'll have more business than you know what to do with.

 Skills necessary: Computer proficiency, the ability to make an accurate diagnosis with few clues, and speed.

 Investment required: Low.

 For more information: Association of Computer Support Specialists, 333 Mamaroneck Avenue #129, White Plains, NY 10605; 914-713-7222; *www.acss.org*

When something goes wrong with a computer, frequently the first inclination is to give it the heave-ho out the window. This is the primary reason that, if you like to tinker with computer innards and tend to be right about the cause of the malady, you should work as hard as you can to get your computer repair business in front of the people who will need it most: frustrated users. They will be glad to have you take it off their hands and make it all better, as long as they don't have to.

I bought one of my first computers from a guy who told me to read the DOS manual so I'd know what to do when something went awry. Like most average computer users who know little about what goes on *inside* the computer, I don't have the time or inclination to read the manual, so I started to look for a computer repair guy who would listen to me explain what went wrong, ask a few questions, and then return it to me a day or two later, good as new. I found him.

If you decide to go into computer repair, and if my story is any inclination, there are millions of other people looking for someone just like you, as well.

19. Computer Training

 Description of the business: A business in which someone teaches an individual or a group how to use a particular piece of software.

 Why it's a good business to start if you don't want to work hard anymore: Many people don't want to have to plow through thick manuals to get the information they need; they'd rather have a real human sit next to them and answer any questions they have.

 Skills necessary: You'll need to like people, to be able to teach them using average language and instructions, and to be proficient and quick when learning new software programs.

 Investment required: Low.

 For more information: Independent Computer Consultants Association, 11131 South Towne Square, St. Louis, MO 63123; 800-774-4222; *www.icca.org*

If you like to teach people new skills and are comfortable with the ins and outs of using and configuring new software programs, you should know there are millions of people out there who would love to have you sit with them and bring them through the steps of learning a new piece of software.

In time, you'll come to think of yourself as a personal trainer for people with computers. Training that's specific to a much-needed skill has already begun to explode in everything from karate to craftmaking, but the biggest need by far is for competent computer teachers, whether you prefer to work one-on-one or to hold court in front of a group.

Though many corporations are now hiring full-time staff trainers, you'll feel freer and make more money by opening your own computer training business. Once word gets around, you should have no trouble finding clients. Besides marketing their businesses with advertising and fliers, many trainers work in tandem with local computer shops, offering to serve as an outside trainer for the shop's clients. After the first visit, you can tell clients you're available to work with them again whenever they acquire a new piece of software, or want to take advantage of the power in their current programs by having you teach them an advanced private class, so to speak.

20. Corporate Test Administration

 Description of the business: A company that plans, acquires, administrates, and evaluates tests for other businesses and their employees as well as prospective hires.

 Why it's a good business to start if you don't want to work hard anymore: Testing is becoming so specialized that it's difficult for a manager or business owner to administer the appropriate tests or even know where to find them. As a result, they will increasingly be looking to outside sources to take care of all of their testing tasks.

 Skills necessary: You'll need to know where to find required tests for specific departments (most often human resources) assist employees, and analyze the outcome to present to the employer.

 Investment required: Medium.

 For more information: American Training & Seminar Association, National Resource & Training Services, 365 South Ocoee Street, Cleveland, TN 37311; 866-572-0142; *www.americantsa.com*

More and more, businesses are relying on a barrage of tests to help them weed out undesirable potential employees and help current employees live up to their potential. With new studies and research appearing daily, a person with a business to run will find it impossible to know where to turn, let alone administer the proper tests.

That's where a corporate test administrator steps in, armed with tests for every conceivable occasion and the resources to help the business owner decide what to do with the results. Nowadays, tests can be given in person, through the mail, and even administered online. Corporate test administrators need to keep up on the newest developments in personality tests and psychological indicators, and they may also be called upon to administer drug and alcohol tests, which may require working with people who are reluctant to cooperate.

Fortune 500 companies have entire departments devoted to test administration. However, 99 percent of American businesses are not as fortunate. They'll be especially receptive to hearing how you can help them to not only take some work off their hands, but advise them on how to help employees be the best they can be, which will help to grow their business.

Corporate test administrators will become an increasingly important part of the corporate landscape in the very near future. If this field appeals to you, your opportunities will be wide open.

21. Courier Service

 Description of the business: A service that delivers documents, packages, and other materials door-to-door.

 Why it's a good business to start if you don't want to work hard anymore: Despite the ease of e-mail and fax, and the proliferation of overnight delivery services, some papers and items still have to be hand-delivered, whether it's across town or to the other side of the world.

 Skills necessary: You should be well-organized and be able to react on the fly because clients will frequently make requests that appear, on the surface, to be impossible to fulfill.

 Investment required: Medium.

? **For more information:** The Association of Messenger Services, 270 Madison Avenue, New York, NY 10016; 212-532-8980

"When it absolutely positively has to be there overnight..." well, FedEx's famous slogan isn't good enough for some businesses and individuals who need their packages delivered before the day is out. But while some courier services operate primarily with an armada of bicycle messengers who spend their days dodging traffic and darting in and out of elevators, others are one-person businesses that operate within a 300-mile radius of their home base and use a car, van, or truck as their mode of transportation.

If you decide to start a courier service, there are a number of decisions

you'll need to make: your delivery area, the kind of transportation you'll use, the range of delivery times you'll use as estimates, and even the industry you'll specialize in, if any. For instance, some courier services specialize in making deliveries for medical supply companies and physicians; they need to equip their vehicles with either a portable cooler or a fixed refrigeration unit due to the instability of specimens and certain drugs when subjected to heat. Other fields have their own particular requirements.

Once you decide on the specifics, if you need to hire others to handle the deliveries while you deal with taking phone calls from clients and parceling out jobs, you'll need to figure out if they will come on board as employees or independent contractors. The latter is the easiest in terms of payment—you pay a commission on each successful delivery—but it may raise some red flags in the eyes of the I.R.S. because they may appear to be employees, and the tax authorities are particularly focused on courier services and the use of independent contractors. Consult with an accountant for the best route to take for your courier service.

22. Crafts Making

 Description of the business: An individual makes a particular line of crafts and sells them at retail outlets, wholesale, on consignment, and at craft shows.

 Why it's a good business to start if you don't want to work hard anymore: Hand-crafted items have always been in demand and will continue to grow in popularity as people continue to appreciate items that show they were made by hand, not machine.

 Skills necessary: If you've been making crafts all your life and specialize in a high-quality item that stands apart from the crowd, you'll increase your chances of success.

 Investment required: Low.

 For more information: *The Crafts Business Answer Book and Resource Guide,* by Barbara Brabec (M. Evans, 1998).

The secret to being successful in the crafts business isn't any different from other businesses: You must anticipate what the market needs and then fill it. The corollary is that if you make what you like, your passion will show through in the finished item, and people will want it because it's obvious it was handcrafted with lots of love.

Both of these seemingly contradictory statements are entirely true when it comes to starting a crafts business. Do what you love; get it out there and in the appropriate outlets, such as crafts shops, shows, and directly to consumers via the web; and then tweak it as necessary. This is one business where it's important to keep tabs on what your competitors are doing, so the next time you go to a crafts show as an observer, not an exhibitor, it's a good idea to play James Bond: Keep an eye on what's selling, which booths are mobbed, what customers are carrying around in their arms. Also keep an eye out for local materials and resources; not only will they cost you less money—if birch trees are endemic to your area, your costs for that material  will be close to nil—but you'll also play up the *native* aspect with your crafts, which is important if your primary market consists of tourists.

Craftspeople who work directly with stores and shopkeepers can sell on consignment or sell direct at wholesale. Some store owners prefer to work one way over another, but you'll get a larger percentage of the sale price if you agree to sell on consignment because the shop owner doesn't need to lay out any money to purchase the item wholesale—his only cost is the display space. Because of this lack of financial commitment, the owner usually pays more to the crafts maker when the item sells. The downside is that while the products are on display, waiting to be purchased, the maker may have lost the chance to display and sell the items in another venue.

23. Custom Clothing Design

 Description of the business: An entrepreneur creates customized clothes and outfits for men and women, for both leisure and the office.

 Why it's a good business to start if you don't want to work hard anymore: More people are choosing clothing that best fits their lifestyle, coloring, and personality, and they can afford to hire a designer who will incorporate all of these specifications into their wardrobe.

 Skills necessary: A background in clothing design and fashion is essential, and a stint with a major designer will help attract attention.

 Investment required: Medium.

 For more information: Professional Association of Custom Clothiers, 6491 Summer Cloud Way, Columbia, MD 21045; 443-755-0303; *www.paccprofessionals.org*

Although it may sound like the ultimate luxury, an increasing number of people are hiring clothing designers to create anywhere from one item of clothing to an entire wardrobe for their personal and professional lives. They are also turning to these professionals for advice on the best clothing for a particular occasion or event.

Clothing designers frequently work with individuals, although more corporations are hiring them to work with executives who may be in the public eye and need to present themselves in a favorable light. In addition, independent designers are called upon to provide personal shopping and wardrobe consulting services or to design and sew one stellar outfit from scratch that could provide a number of totally different looks when paired with different clothes and accessories. The personal shopping realm is how many clothing designers initially enter the business, if indeed they do have a background in the field.

Some custom clothing designers work with clients all over the country, using measurements and photographs provided by the customer, while others prefer to work with their clients in person, at least for the first meeting or two. In this cutthroat business, going out on your own and working one-on-one with clients could also be easier and more satisfying than striving to be the next Donna Karan, who probably spends more time running the business end of her design franchise than on actually designing next season's line. If you love clothes, know how to design and fit them, and know what looks stylish and current, this may be the dream career for you.

24. Customized Computer Business

Description of the business: A business that sells and sets up the best specific hardware, software, and network equipment for a particular small business and offers tech support and house calls as a matter of course.

Why it's a good business to start if you don't want to work hard anymore: More people prefer to rely on one source for their computer systems, from purchasing the equipment to calling when the system breaks down. It saves time and money because the specialist installed the system, and is already familiar with it.

Skills necessary: Computer proficiency is assumed. However, it's also important to be familiar with the quirks of a particular business, whether it's a specific industry, the size of the company, security issues and access, and/or the physical layout of the office.

Investment required: High.

For more information: National Computer Association, 13555 Automobile Boulevard, Clearwater, FL 33762; 727-785-0414; *www.ncavars.com*

If you've always wanted to be someone's knight in shining armor, then starting a customized computer business is just about the best chance around. When it comes to computers, many businesspeople are less than knowledgeable about the mechanics, but they easily become frustrated when dealing with distant or inaccessible tech support or with hardware and software companies that are unfamiliar with the specifics of their industry.

Customized computer specialists come in many different stripes, because many choose to focus their service on one narrow field—such as real estate or medical practices, for instance—but there are generalists, as well. In fact, one rapidly growing market segment consists of small businesses and offices.

Here's the advantage: This service does it all. Businesspeople no longer have to call one support line when the software crashes and another when the printer freezes up. Customized computer specialists can offer convenience, know-how, and service that's usually a lot quicker than their customers would get from a faceless voice on a toll-free support line.

If you prefer to work with a set number of clients who you can really get to know and have the patience to work with them, this is the way to go.

25. Database Management

 Description of the business: A company that sets up and maintains databases for other businesses.

 Why it's a good business to start if you don't want to work hard anymore: Although more businesses are using databases for purposes of inventory, marketing, accounting, and personnel (among other uses), many don't have a full-time database manager on staff to help the company use the data to its full potential. That's where a contracted database management service comes in.

 Skills necessary: You'll need to be familiar with data modeling processes and be able to analyze a particular industry's need for a variety of databases.

 Investment required: Medium.

? **For more information:** Data Management Association, PO Box 5786, Bellevue, WA 98006; 425-562-2636; *www.dama.org*

In this information-is-king society of ours, those people who know how to present statistics, numbers, and other information of a business in a way that shows employees and interested outsiders the relational health of a business will be indispensable to that company. The problem is that there aren't too many people out there who are able to take raw figures and have them make sense as they relate to each other.

Database managers can help streamline the job of everyone at the company. For instance, a database manager can design a database that ties in with a company's accounting database so that every time one widget is sold, it is automatically subtracted from the company's inventory database.

In turn, the inventory database can be set so that when the widget inventory reaches a certain number, a message is sent to notify the buyer to purchase more widgets in order to keep the inventory from falling to critically low levels.

While this may sound like something a computer programmer could do, database management requires a familiarity with the inner workings of a company as well as knowledge of that particular industry. The demand for database managers far exceeds the supply, making this business a surefire bet if you meet the criteria.

26. Daycare

 Description of the business: A service that provides care for kids of all ages in a private home or separate facility.

 Why it's a good business to start if you don't want to work hard anymore: We'll never return to the traditional nuclear family scenario, but Americans will still keep having kids. Competent and kindhearted caregivers are needed to take care of children while their parents are working. This is the perfect business if you think getting paid to spend the day with little kids is your idea of heaven.

 Skills necessary: You'll need a background in childhood education, a passion for teaching, and a strong sense of diplomacy when dealing with parents.

 Investment required: Medium.

? **For more information:** *Start & Run a Home Daycare,* by Catherine M. Pruissen (Self-Counsel Press, 2003).

If kids are our future, daycare is the vehicle that will get them there safely and sanely. It's no secret that caring, competent caregivers are few and far between, so if you have a passion for kids and love to see them learn, starting a daycare business is a great way for you to go.

Kids are often watched over in the provider's own home, which in most cases must be approved and licensed by a state agency. Preschool-aged kids will stay all day, while school-age children may come before school starts as well as after school. One growing area of childcare is on-site daycare, provided mostly by large corporations and businesses, and offered most frequently as an employee benefit, partly subsidized by the company. The facility may be co-owned or run by an individual entrepreneur.

Many providers get started by opening daycare centers in their own homes and taking in a few kids on a part-time basis—certainly the most inexpensive route to go. It's possible to open a center in a separate building, but many entrepreneurs who are new to the daycare business will want to test the waters and build up the clientele list by starting small. Once word gets around that the kids love being with you and your staff and their parents feel good about leaving their children in your care, you're free to expand at will.

27. Desktop Publishing

 Description of the business: A company that designs promotional materials, advertisements, resumes, publications, and other documents for businesses and consumers.

 Why it's a good business to start if you don't want to work hard anymore: Despite the proliferation of easy-to-use graphic-design and page-layout software, many businesspeople don't have the time or simply prefer to contract out this work to experienced professionals.

 Skills necessary: Computer proficiency and experience in commercial art and graphic design, as well as copy editing, all help.

 Investment required: Medium.

 For more information: *How to Start a Home-Based Desktop Publishing Business,* by Louise Kursmark (Globe Pequot Press, 1999).

The widespread development and use of desktop publishing programs that seem to be able to do everything but wash the windows has resulted in a steep increase in the number of people—entrepreneurs and employees alike—who can whip out anything their company may need in the way of marketing materials and written documents.

The problem? Not everyone has the time or desire to produce these documents, and fewer still have the eye for graphics and the talent with words that are vital to make them stand out. The U.S. Bureau of Labor Statistics predicts that the number of full-time desktop publishing jobs within companies will increase 74 percent by 2006. A person who starts a desktop publishing service will be able to see his business jump by a similar percentage.

Despite the computer revolution, the majority of Americans remain computer-phobic, yet they still need the kinds of materials and documents a desktop publisher can produce quickly and easily. Therefore, one of the most important skills you can have as a desktop publisher is to be a great listener, and be able to ask the questions that bring precise answers and will result in the high-quality product your customer expects.

The best way to get started is to approach companies you already do business with and offer your services. Perhaps they've wanted a new brochure or advertisements for awhile, but haven't yet gotten around to it. Because the majority of businesses don't keep a full-time graphic designer on staff, especially small retail stores and service providers, your services would be perfect for them.

28. Distance Teaching

 Description of the business: A business that provides instruction to students no matter where they live. This could consist of adult-school courses, college classes, and professional-level licensing instruction.

 Why it's a good business to start if you don't want to work hard anymore: Many people would take outside classes or even postsecondary courses if the time and place were right. Distance education allows people to attend classes and submit papers 24 hours a day.

 Skills necessary: You'll need to love to teach, know your subject matter inside out, and be able to motivate students from afar.

 Investment required: Medium.

 For more information:
American Center for the Study of Distance Education
Pennsylvania State University, College of Education
411 Keller Building, University Park, PA 16802;
814-863-3764; *www.ed.psu.edu/acsde*

Americans have always thirsted for knowledge, whether it's out of curiosity or to further their careers. In the past, they've been limited to attending classes in a central location, but technology has opened up a vast world in the form of distance education. And while students are the most obvious beneficiaries, teachers, who may have been limited by their location, can now teach for community schools, colleges, and universities all over the world.

Better yet, many teachers are actually starting their own distance schools in a specific discipline, such as fiction writing or coaching for civil service exams, and pursuing students through online and traditional means. However, if you start your distance-teaching business by signing on with an accredited school, you'll technically be running your own business because the school will probably consider you to be an independent contractor, and not an employee.

Distance learning is just starting to catch on, both among students and teachers. The use of interactive video, chats, and e-mail between teacher and students, and Web pages used to post assignments and tests mean that learning is now limitless, as is your distance education business.

29. Dog Walking

 Description of the business: A service where a person walks one or more dogs every day, twice a day, usually during the week while the pet owners are at work.

 Why it's a good business to start if you don't want to work hard anymore: People are pampering pets more, and feel guilty that they're left alone during the day. In an urban area, a dog walker will find many eager clients. Due to its periodic nature, you'll be busy for a few hours a couple of times a day, mostly during the week, and then have the rest of the time for yourself.

 Skills necessary: You'll need to be comfortable working with dogs, and be attuned to the signals and moods that dogs can throw off.

 Investment required: Low.

 For more information: *Dog & Kennel Magazine,* Pet Business Inc., 7-L Dundas Circle, Greensboro, NC 27407; 336-292-4047; *www.dogandkennel.com*

Even though many kids thought that walking the family dog was akin to taking out the garbage, many of those same kids are probably now adults who would love the idea of getting paid to walk the dog. Maybe you're even one of them.

Indeed, dog walking seems to be one of those businesses that's just too good to be true, except on exceptionally cold, wet, and windy days. But even then, with the proliferation of wagging tails and the assorted bays and barks, if you were obligated to take a pack of dogs on a brisk walk through a winter wonderland, well, as the lone human at the beck and call of a pack of clowns whose job it is to make you laugh and forget the world, you might not even notice the weather.

One of the best parts of being a dog walker is that you're working with a crowd of living creatures who are always overjoyed to see you. I'd chal-lenge you to name even one human who you can say the same of. Some dog walkers escort a maximum of five dogs at a time, while others are hearty enough to handle 10. It's easy to find clients; on the weekends, hang out in your local park and blithely ask any dog owners you see who cares for the dog when they're at work. Put a notice at the local veterinarian's office as well as the pet shop. You can also make up a jacket displaying the words *"DOG WALKING OUR SPECIALTY"* on the back, along with your phone number and/or e-mail address. In no time at all, your services will be in demand, and you won't be able to keep the hounds at bay.

30. E-commerce Consulting

 Description of the business: A consultant works with entrepreneurs and companies to determine how to use the Web and Internet to sell and market their existing products and services.

 Why it's a good business to start if you don't want to work hard anymore: Most companies understand that they need to be online, although they don't always know how to effectively conduct business once there. An e-commerce expert can help develop plans and strategies for online companies.

 Skills necessary: You'll need to have proven yourself in online commerce, or at least have a rudimentary understanding of how business is successfully conducted online.

 Investment required: Medium.

 For more information: *The e-Business Formula for Success,* by Susan Sweeney (Maximum Press, 2002).

Since its early days, e-commerce has drawn a lot of interest from businesses of all stripes. However, many companies that threw up a rudimentary Web page thought they could just sit back and wait for the orders to roll in.

Today, businesses know this is not the case, but they still couldn't say for sure what works online and what doesn't. An e-commerce specialist with some background in building a successful commercial Website will have more work than she can handle, due to the clamoring of

CFOs and Webmasters everywhere who are looking for the magic formula that will bring in the bucks.

An e-commerce consultant needs to have a foot in two diametrically opposed worlds: traditional commerce and the head-butting Internet. Although an e-commerce consultant is frequently called upon to offer an opinion on the best shopping cart program on the market, the work tends to be more esoteric than this. Instead, the ability to analyze Website design and layout, ease of loading pages, and even knowing which products to feature on the site all come into play, typically with equal importance.

In the eyes of corporate America, e-commerce is still pioneer land. Savvy marketing experts who want to be able to write the rules and buck the trends while frequently working within the establishment, well, here is your chance.

In the wild and wooly world of the Internet, it's a rare business that doesn't have some kind of Web presence. However, a business that is making a hefty profit from its Website can be equally rare, because few understand how to turn an online store into a profitable branch.

31. Educational Consulting

 Description of the business: A professional provides consultations on the variety of educational possibilities for a child, whether it's a private school, four-year college, or summer camp.

 Why it's a good business to start if you don't want to work hard anymore: Whether dealing with financial aid or the most appropriate school, an educational consultant can help parents sort out the wheat from the chaff and point them to resources they may not know about. You can run this business by meeting with parents in person or by consulting over the Internet. In either case, many parents are willing to pay big bucks for the best advice for their children.

 Skills necessary: A background in education and/or childhood counseling helps, as does a talent for conducting in-depth research.

 Investment required: Low.

For more information: Independent Educational Consultants Association, 3251 Old Lee Highway, Suite 510, Fairfax, VA 22030; 703-591-4850; *www.educationalconsulting.org*

Education is globally recognized as the key to success for everyone from infants to senior citizens, regardless of their backgrounds. However, people who are investigating the variety of possibilities don't always know where to look for the information they need.

Parents don't have the time to sift through complicated financial aid applications, and few have the desire to do the necessary research to determine why X College would be a better environment for their child than Y College. That's where the educational consultant comes in. These professionals can help frazzled parents and their children narrow down their choices for schools as well as point them to sources of financial aid and scholarships that few people may know about.

But this is only one of several fields in educational consulting today. Another area is one in which a consultant serves as a kind of freelance counselor for a troubled teen, serving as a sympathetic shoulder for a kid who feels neither his parents nor his teachers really listen to him. Another area of specialty for educational consultants includes acting as a mediator between two divorcing parents, whose rage often interferes with the coolheadedness that knows, in calmer times, what the best choice is for the child.

In the future, educational consultants will undoubtedly branch out to other areas, including counseling adult students, working in tandem with corporations that pay for education for employees, and even helping to guide distance learners. People love to learn; as such, educational consultants will continue to grow as a viable and influential source of information for people who want to know where their best opportunities lie.

32. Elder Concierge Service

 Description of the business: This is a business that caters to people over age 55, helping them to perform their daily errands, transporting them to functions, and stepping in as a go-between to extract improved service from government and private agencies when necessary.

 Why it's a good business to start if you don't want to work hard anymore: Americans are getting older. As they live longer lives, they find they are no longer able to do all of the things they once were able to do on their own, so a concierge can come in handy. You can run the errands for clients in the course of doing your own.

 Skills necessary: You'll need patience and the desire to work with older people, as well as the research skills to ferret out the places to get information and assistance.

 Investment required: Low.

 For more information: *The Concierge Manual, Second Edition,* by Katharine C. Giovanni (NewRoad Publishing, 2002).

These days, any new business that offers a specific and much-needed service to a particular group of people is bound to succeed. That goes for corporate executives, dog lovers, and even people over the age of 55.

The idea of hiring a concierge who specializes in working with senior citizens is a new idea whose time has definitely come. Think of it: If a retired woman has the time to do the kinds of things she wants to do and the money to hire somebody to do the things she doesn't want to do, well, why shouldn't that person be you? It's true that the senior could always hire a specialized service to do the dirty work, but a concierge is able to present a variety of services all wrapped up in one package. Besides, concierges specialize in offering information to people and knowing where to turn for that special service or product when no one else can find it.

However, the clientele of an elder concierge is not at all limited to people of means. Just knowing how to cut through the red tape of government aging and medical agencies will mean you're providing a valuable service for people who would probably rather let things slide than take action. If you love working with older people and getting stellar results, maybe you should try billing yourself as an elder concierge. Your customers will love you for it.

33. Elder Daycare

 Description of the business: A service that offers care providers and companions for senior citizens, in an independent facility and/or in the senior's own home.

 Why it's a good business to start if you don't want to work hard anymore: Americans are living longer lives, and while they lose some ability to carry on with their lives, most don't need to move to a nursing home either. Elder daycare fills in the gaps, allowing seniors to stay in their own homes while providing them with the company and care they need.

 Skills necessary: A nursing background or experience as a home health aide is helpful.

 Investment required: Medium to high.

 For more information: Assisted Living Federation of America, 11200 Waples Mill Road, Suite 150, Fairfax VA 22030; 703-691-8100; *www.alfa.org*

Baby Boomers are getting older, and so are their parents. More seniors want to stay in their homes as long as they can, which means they'll need more specialists to help them accomplish this goal. While medical experts can help fill the need on the health side, when it comes to daily care and companionship, the field is wide open for individuals and services who can provide guidance and activities for seniors, whether it's in their own homes or in a separate daycare facility.

In many ways, elder daycare follows the same formula as daycare for kids: Combine a few fun activities with a meal or two, set aside  some time for adequate rest, and everyone is happy. A one-person business can accomplish this by working in a senior's own private home, or staffs can do it by running elder daycare programs in separate facilities, which are often run and organized—or at least provided with supplemental operational funding—by governmental agencies, whether local, county, or state. As with daycare aimed at children, there are a number of hurdles to cross when it comes to setting up a freestanding facility. For this reason, the majority of people interested in becoming elder daycare providers choose in-home private care, in the senior's own home, or in some cases, in the provider's home.

34. Elder Taxi Service

 Description of the business: A service that provides door-to-door transportation for senior citizens, bringing them to doctor's appointments, friend's homes, and senior centers.

 Why it's a good business to start if you don't want to work hard anymore: As Americans age, they are living longer in their own homes, but they may not be able to drive as much as they used to. A service that will bring them to the places they need to go should thrive. And if you already do a lot of driving and like to have people along for the ride, this business is a good choice.

 Skills necessary: You'll need to have good rapport with people of an older generation and a clean driving record is requisite.

 Investment required: Medium.

 For more information: Community Transportation Association of America, 1341 G Street NW, 10th Floor, Washington, DC 20005; 202-628-1480; *www.ctaa.org*

As people grow older and retire, many are not following in the footsteps of their predecessors and moving to Florida; indeed, many are choosing to remain in their own homes. For those seniors who are located in suburban and rural areas where public transportation is sometimes not readily available, savvy entrepreneurs are starting taxi services that exclusively cater to this age group.

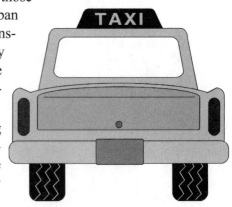

More Americans are living longer, although their ability to successfully operate a motor vehicle has a good chance of significantly decreasing as they enter their 70s and 80s. Experts point out that the lack of mobility often results in depression and, therefore, a shorter lifespan. A personalized taxi service for senior citizens can help them regain most of their mobility and make their years happy and healthy ones.

If you're considering starting a taxi service for seniors, you'll have the best chances for success in an area with a significant graying population and where the local public transportation systems leave a lot to be desired. A study conducted by the U.S. Conference of Mayors and the National Association of Counties projected that more than 75 percent of Americans over the age of 65 are living in suburban and rural areas where adequate forms of public transportation are sorely lacking. You may need to buy or lease a specially-equipped van with a wheelchair lift, but if a good portion of your customer base consists of driving seniors to the local subsidized senior center, you may be able to get the local aging council to help offset the cost of both the van and the special equipment.

35. Electronic Publishing Consulting

Description of the business: A consultant works with companies to determine the design, content, and appropriateness of creating or converting documents to electronic formats.

Why it's a good business to start if you don't want to work hard anymore: Like e-commerce, corporate America doesn't have a hold on how electronic publishing differs from traditional publishing, and they don't know when to employ it. An experienced consultant can help lead the way.

Skills necessary: A publishing background helps, whether in content, design, or both.

Investment required: Medium.

For more information: *Electronic Publishing: The Definitive Guide,* by Karen S. Wiesner (Hard Shell Word Factory, 2003).

Many pundits claim that electronic publishing will eventually do away with the printed page, and whether or not you agree, electronic publishing is quickly becoming a stand-alone form of communication in some arenas, while in others it is considered to be a supplement, or a replacement for convenience.

Electronic publishing isn't just the Web; it's writing and marketing electronic business, automated e-mail replies when a potential customer requests more information, even broadcast fax, e-mail, and pages designed to deliver information the instant it's transmitted.

However, electronic publishing is much more than converting print publications to digital form. In order to take advantage of its impatient reputation, everything needs to be different to satisfy the electronic customer. As an electronic publishing consultant, you'll help corporations alter their message for these new formats, changing design, content, focus, everything.

The market for electronic publishing consultants is bright; even after the *Fortune* 500 and their ilk master the art and recognize the need for ongoing e-publishing, your work has just begun, whether it's finding the talented writers and designers for the contracted assignments you receive or recommending a complete overhaul for the company's current roster of digitally delivered documents. We'll still have to kill trees to impart information, but electronic publishing consultants will be in the forefront when it comes to helping smooth the transition and take advantage of a market that's faster, easier, and cheaper for companies everywhere to reach.

36. Employee Recruiting

 Description of the business: A service that contracts with businesses to locate and screen competent prospective employees.

 Why it's a good business to start if you don't want to work hard anymore: Even when unemployment rates climb, companies will still need a fresh influx of talented employees in particular fields and will outsource the work to agencies. If you specialize in a certain industry or job category, it's easier to build your contacts. Because you work on commission when placing an employee, if you deal with high-salaried workers, your hourly rate could be significant.

 Skills necessary: You should be comfortable making cold calls to both companies and employees. You should be a skilled interviewer and be able to make an instinctive decision about a prospective employee's ability to fit the job description and the company.

 Investment required: Medium.

 For more information: Recruiters Online Network, 3325 Landershire Lane, Suite 1001, Plano, TX 75023; 888-821-2490; *www.recruitersonline.com*

If you are thinking about opening up shop as a recruiter, you must know that both employers and employees will hate you and love you at some point; employers will snub you if it's clear you're trying to lure away one of their star employees, while employees will frown at you if you are unable to promise to find them their dream job.

On the flip side, employers will love you if you take the difficult and time-consuming job of finding and qualifying employees off their hands, and employees will be enamored of you if you're able to convince a potential employer to meet all their needs. The unofficial recruiter's motto: You win some, you lose some. The best recruiters are consummate jugglers.

Of any of the fields in this book, recruitment is truly a feast-or-famine situation, with the current economic climate dictating which group you're more popular with. When the unemployment rate is low, employers are begging you for new employees; when unemployment is higher, employees will be knocking on your door.

Persistence and tact definitely pay off; a recruiter may pull in as much as 50 percent of the first-year salary of a newly-hired employee. With these odds, it's clear that recruiters are willing to lose a lot in order to win a few.

37. Employee Training

 Description of the business: A business that trains corporate employees in everything from new computer programs to incorporating diversity and even creativity into the workplace.

 Why it's a good business to start if you don't want to work hard anymore: Corporations will turn to outside trainers more frequently for the specialized experience these professionals can bring to sessions; retaining a staff trainer who's a generalist in nature will increasingly be frowned upon. This specialty business can command stellar fees.

 Skills necessary: You should be an informative and entertaining teacher and know your subject matter inside out.

 Investment required: Medium.

For more information: American Society for Training and Development, 1640 King Street, Alexandria, VA 22313; 703-683-8100; *www.astd.org*

It's becoming increasingly difficult for businesses and their employees to keep up with the new developments, released almost daily, that will help workers to perform their jobs better and stay focused to boot.

While much of the attention paid to employee training is on the computer side, corporations are beginning to pay attention to training employees in areas that range from effective communication and customer relations to stress management. Corporations also realize that it doesn't make sense to have an armada of trainers on staff, but that it's better to bring in real specialists as the need arises. The best trainers are able to shift gears when it's obvious that a particular employee isn't responding to a particular technique. In-house trainers might be more likely to toe the corporate line than break ranks, while outside consultants would bear no such allegiance, and as a result, be a little more outrageous, which tends to be more effective in helping employees to improve retention and learn new skills than boring talks and seminars in which instructors drone on for hours.

Many of the best employee trainers are frustrated actors, and it shows. If you've always dreamed of Broadway but would settle for a slightly smaller audience, as long as you are able to get your point across and your audience is happy to learn a few things from you while having fun, then perhaps starting a business as a corporate trainer is a good choice for you.

38. Entrepreneurial Consulting

 Description of Business: A service that trains people to start and run their own businesses and provides advice to entrepreneurs who have been in business for a year or longer.

 Why it's a good business to start if you don't want to work hard anymore: Well, you're reading this book, aren't you? Starting a business is the new American dream, which means there will be many more people who will need help getting started and keeping it going. And they're willing to pay for it, even if you consult on a remote basis.

 Skills necessary: A background in running your own business helps. You'll also need to have a talent for asking probing questions and for coaching your clients to follow up on the advice you give them.

 Investment required: Low.

 For more information: Your local Small Business Administration office and SCORE (Service Corps of Retired Executives) chapters.

If you ask the next 10 strangers you meet if they're thinking about starting their own businesses, chances are that you'll receive affirmative answers from at least eight of them. As corporate America has squeezed the enthusiasm out of its workers, more people are deciding to break ranks and be in control by starting their own business. Many of these people will buy a book or tape on how to proceed, and subscribe to one of the many entrepreneurial publications available.

This is the point at which many will get bogged down. They'll either not know exactly how to proceed or what it is they want to do, or they may just think they don't have what it takes to start their own venture.

That's where you come in as an entrepreneurial consultant. You can show people with the entrepreneurial bug exactly what they need to do to get started, how to narrow their target audience, even provide them with an hour of coaching each week to pepper you with questions and ask for advice, much like a therapist would. Entrepreneurial consultants work on both an individual basis and conduct seminars or classes through local community schools in order to build up a list of potential clients. Obviously you'll have more credibility as an entrepreneurial consultant if you've already started and run at least one business, but even if you've tried and failed, you have experience under your belt that entrepreneurial novices wish they had.

39. Errand Service

 Description of the business: A service that runs errands for consumers and businesses, which may include everything from dropping off the dry cleaning to renewing a passport.

 Why it's a good business to start if you don't want to work hard anymore: The most precious resource people have today is time. If they can hire somebody else to run errands for them on a regular basis, they'll have more time for the things they want to do.

 Skills necessary: You'll need to be well-organized, patient, and know where to find answers and resources quickly.

 Investment required: Low.

For more information: *How to Start and Operate an Errand Service,* by Rob Spina (Legacy Marketing, 2001).

If you consider yourself to be a jack- or jill-of-all-trades and like the idea of providing a useful service to people who will really appreciate your efforts, you should consider the idea of starting a business where you run errands for other people.

An errand service actually incorporates a number of the other businesses described in this book, and is ideal for aspiring entrepreneurs who like to have a variety of chores to perform and are good at juggling. For example, in the course of one day, you may be called upon by clients to walk a dog, buy a birthday present for a relative, sweep the walk, and go grocery shopping.

The future looks extremely bright for errand services because people with more money than time are getting used to the idea of paying somebody else to perform the tasks that they would rather not spend the time on. And once they hire you to do one chore for them, as they see how easy it is and how it frees up their time, your clients are very likely to hire you to run even more errands for them. The good news is that many of the errands that you'll perform for multiple clients can be piggybacked so that you end up spending very little extra time running more errands even though the number of clients has increased.

An errand service is a great business for the 21st century. After all, how could a harried executive resist the motto, "We'll run ourselves ragged for you"?

40. E-zine Publishing

 Description of the business: A company that produces and markets a business or magazine via e-mail or on the Internet.

 Why it's a good business to start if you don't want to work hard anymore: People are increasingly relying on electronic delivery methods to receive information in a given field, whether career- or hobby-related. If you specialize in publishing electronically, you can either produce your own publication or publish an e-zine for another company.

 Skills necessary: You should be familiar with how to slant and write content for e-zines, and a background in traditional writing and publishing helps. However, computer proficiency is equally important.

 Investment required: Medium.

 For more information: "The Handbook of E-Zine Publishing," by Kate Schultz; *www.e-zinez.com/handbook/index.html*

An e-zine is a publication that takes after its namesake, a magazine, but is published easier, cheaper, and more quickly via e-mail or the Internet.

There are two distinct ways to go: Publish an e-zine yourself and make it available for free to anyone who asks (in which case you'll have to sell advertising in order to pay the bills) or contract yourself out to write and design one for another company, which may choose to use it as a promotional vehicle for their business and transmit it to their customer base for free.

Another method of e-zine publishing is to charge a subscription fee, although this usually works best with existing publications that want to convert all or part of their readership to a paperless format.

As is the case with other technical businesses, you may need to spend time convincing prospective clients of the need for your services and that their customers would probably welcome the option to receive information in an electronic format. But the sky is truly the limit when it comes to the potential opportunities for producing e-zines—either your own or for other companies.

41. Financial Planning for Seniors

 Description of the business: A service that provides financial advice and investment suggestions to people who are over the age of 55.

 Why it's a good business to start if you don't want to work hard anymore: The baby-boom generation is graying, and as their investment requirements change with the passing of time, they'll need more specialized advice.

 Skills necessary: A background and certification as a financial planner helps, as well as experience as a stockbroker and a knowledge of tax issues.

 Investment required: Low.

 For more information: Financial Planning Association, 4100 E. Mississippi Avenue, Suite 400, Denver, CO 80246; 800-322-4237; *www.fpanet.org*

Once their kids are grown and out of the house and parents have amassed enough of a portfolio to enable them to retire, a senior's financial needs change, and drastically. The problem is that many traditional financial planners fail to advise their clients to change their investment strategies from earlier in life, which may be too aggressive for a person's golden years.

Enter financial planners who specifically address the needs of clients who no longer have to save for their kids' college years or set aside huge chunks of income every year to ensure a secure retirement. Instead, seniors are all ears when it comes to policies for guaranteed coverage for a nursing home, reverse mortgages, and deferred annuities. If you're interested in pursuing this specialty as a financial planner, you should realize that you have the same options for getting paid as do investment professionals who work with younger investors: You either charge a flat fee or earn a commission on the products you sell. However, you may want to rethink your pricing strategy because a less aggressive investor frequently translates to less stock trading activity and, therefore, fewer and lower commissions with each trade.

In any case, financial planners who decide to cater to older Americans will probably have their hands full, as the number of Baby Boomers turning 50 each day will continue to build well into the future.

42. Food Delivery Service

 Description of the business: A service that contracts with local restaurants to deliver food and meals to offices and residences.

 Why it's a good business to start if you don't want to work hard anymore: People are cooking less. However, the cocooning trend of the 1990s shows that people are also staying home more. Delivering restaurant food to people who prefer to stay home combines the best of both worlds.

 Skills necessary: You'll need to be able to negotiate with restaurants for timely preparation and decent prices in order to offer a wide variety of food to clients.

 Investment required: Medium.

? **For more information:** *Hospitality Sales: A Marketing Approach,* by Margaret Shaw (John Wiley, 1999).

When you imagine the convenience and luxury of having a just-cooked restaurant meal delivered to your door, it's not hard to fathom why the future looks extremely bright for an entrepreneur who decides to start a food delivery service.

Because Americans have become connoisseurs when it comes to cuisine and ethnic foods, the opportunity to offer them more than pizza via home and office delivery will win over many customers. The good news is that you don't even have to be a good cook to start a food delivery service

because you will work with local restaurants that prepare the meals. You're in charge of delivering it to its final destination.

A food delivery service typically works in this fashion: You receive an order for a particular meal, which you then relay to the restaurant. You (or one of your drivers) pick it up, paying the restaurant typically 75 percent of the regular menu price, and then deliver it to the home or office destination, where you charge the full menu price to the customer and add on a delivery surcharge that ranges from $2–$5.

The best markets for a food delivery service are upscale urban neighborhoods and suburbs, office parks, and hotels. All offer a concentrated population of people who are willing to pay to have good meals delivered to their door. And with a food delivery service, it's easy to build up a loyal audience of repeat business. After all, everyone has to eat.

43. Furniture Making

 Description of the business: A craftsperson makes chairs, tables, and other wooden furniture for individuals and retail stores.

 Why it's a good business to start if you don't want to work hard anymore: Handcrafted items of good quality will continue to be in demand in America's mass-production society.

 Skills necessary: Though there's a lot of competition out there, if you've perfected your skills as a hobby and you specialize in one particular period—Shaker or Arts and Crafts, for example—once word gets around, you'll have more business than you can handle.

 Investment required: Low.

For more information: *Fine Woodworking Magazine,* PO Box 5506, Newtown, CT 06470; 203-426-8171; *www.taunton.com*

If you have sawdust in your veins and tend to lose all track of time while working with a lathe to make sure that chair leg has just the right curve to it, then starting a business making hand-crafted furniture would be a good choice for you.

Many hobbies make great businesses, and furniture making is no exception; chances are good that you already have all of the equipment and knowledge you need to get started. But first you'll have to get the word out to your customer base through crafts shows, farmers markets, consignment shops, and other suitable venues. Usually, furniture makers find that word of mouth takes over after the first six months to a year, when commissioned work becomes the bulk of the workload.

The majority of furniture makers prefer to sell their work directly to customers because, when you build furniture by hand, it's difficult to make it inexpensively enough to sell wholesale to a shop that will then double the price but still need to offer it at an affordable rate. By selling direct, a furniture maker can price items at the same level a retail store would charge, but in this case, you'll get to keep all of the money instead of splitting it with the shop.

To determine the price of a chair, a furniture maker estimates the cost of the materials used and adds in the labor on an hourly basis. Depending upon your location, the price of materials, and your overhead and personal bills, a handmade chair can range from $250 to $2,000, and much more, in many instances.

Most furniture makers don't get rich, but they're able to make a living doing the work they love—a great indication that it's a perfect business if you don't want to work hard anymore.

44. Genealogical Research

 Description of the business: A service that helps people to locate long-lost relatives, research the ties between generations, and provide some perspective on a family's roots in the form of a family tree or history.

 Why it's a good business to start if you don't want to work hard anymore: People are more interested in learning about the intricate fabric of their family history. Genealogy is a rapidly-growing industry, but few people have the time and knowledge to conduct a thorough search. If you like spending hours wandering around online just to see what you can find, or to answer a particular question, this will be a great business for you.

 Skills necessary: You must know how to do thorough research, know where to look for obscure facts and documents, and be able to keep the big picture in mind when wrestling with the smaller bits of information.

 Investment required: Low.

For more information: Association of Professional Genealogists, PO Box 350998, Westminster, CO 80035; 303-422-9371; *www.apgen.org*

Genealogy is hot. Just look at the interest in scrapbooking, even though this trend applies more to being able to maintain a complete family history as it happens and not to go back through a couple of centuries in order to get the complete picture on matriarchs, patriarchs, even black sheep. Once someone is hooked on creating a current history, however, chances are good that the bug will bite hard and cause a person to want to know more about his roots. While some people will want to do the whole thing themselves, most people don't have the resources or the time, and they won't know where to look for the information they need.

As a genealogical researcher, you'll be able to consult with curious families in a variety of ways, either by offering to teach them the basics of how to start their research, or by filling in the gaps they are not able to fill. This could include spending a day in the state historical society, writing down the names of publications that are appropriate to their search, or actually leafing through the books and 100-year-old newspaper archives page by page, looking for the names of family members who may be a branch on the family tree.

Of course genealogy is not an exact or a stagnant art. If you love getting up to your elbows in old books and papers and have a passion for witnessing how certain historical events affected one family, you'll be in heaven as a genealogical researcher.

45. Gift Basket Business

 Description of the business: Packaging merchandise in baskets for people to give as gifts. Baskets can be organized around a theme, such as a new home or a baby shower.

 Why it's a good business to start if you don't want to work hard anymore: Many people are too busy to spend much time thinking about the best gift to give for a particular occasion. And giving a basket filled with a variety of items helps increase the chances that the recipient will like it.

 Skills necessary: It helps if you have a flair for design as well as the ability to envision baskets and contents that will stand out.

 Investment required: Low.

 For more information: *Start & Run a Gift Basket Business,* by Mardi Foster-Walker (Self-Counsel Press, 2003).

When it comes to the gift basket business, it helps to think like a florist, always staying one step ahead of the next holiday. Indeed, a gift basket business is a very seasonal business—of course people will order a basket for the obvious occasions, such as birthdays, Mother's Day, and Christmas. The rest of the time, being a creative thinker helps. Successful gift basket entrepreneurs have developed some unusual themed baskets that get attention and are easily sold because they are so different: baskets for golfers, one for a dog that's just had puppies, or a basket filled with items that are used in age-old, erotic Kama Sutra practices.

Gift basket entrepreneurs can work independently, providing baskets on an as-ordered basis, or create baskets for local stores to sell. Another outlet is to make up a variety of baskets in advance and then sign up for a booth at local crafts shows and fairs, or even rent a small booth at a local crafts mall.

Starting a gift basket business is easy and limitless because the market for your baskets is limited only to your imagination. The only downside is that in order to make a decent profit in the business it's necessary to order supplies from wholesale dealers, who usually require a minimum order of $250 or more. However, many new gift basket businesses take off quickly from the first day their doors are open, hit the ground running, and run through their first batch of inventory in no time at all.

46. Global Marketplace Consulting

Description of the business: A businessperson who works with other businesses to help them determine if their products and/or services will translate to overseas markets, and if so, the best ways to reach them.

Why it's a good business to start if you don't want to work hard anymore: With the growth of the Internet and the increase in labor costs in the United States, even the smallest companies are interested in doing business with overseas companies, but most need an expert to guide them.

Skills necessary: A background in international commerce and excellent research skills help. You'll need to understand protocol and etiquette in foreign countries.

Investment required: Medium.

For more information: *The Borderless World: Power and Strategy in the Interlinked Economy,* by Kenichi Ohmae (HarperBusiness, 1999).

The world is getting smaller, at least when it comes to conducting business. Nowadays entrepreneurs in all industries think nothing of including the entire world in their marketing plans, while a few years ago, it wasn't even on their radar screens.

Becoming a global marketing consultant requires the skill of an actor, the familiarity with a variety of cultures, and an inordinate amount of patience. Obviously it's a great help to have a strong background in the field and lots of experience. However, it's not necessary to even have your passport up to date; you can limit your practice to consulting with American entrepreneurs about the realities of the global marketplace, as it applies to their industry, and lay out a blueprint for them to follow. Or you can serve as their ambassador overseas, representing the company in all of its foreign business dealings: negotiating contracts, schmoozing with company honchos—in short, doing everything necessary to bring the negotiations to the point so that all the U.S.-based company head has to do is sign the paper in order to commit to the deal.

Global marketing consultants can work on an hourly or a per diem basis, though the more savvy among them will take a reduced fee or none in exchange for a percentage of the total amount of the final deal. After all, these guys know how to negotiate.

47. Gourmet Food Store

Description of the business: A specialty shop that focuses on high-end products that typically aren't readily available in supermarkets.

Why it's a good business to start if you don't want to work hard anymore: People are becoming more discriminating when it comes to the foods they eat. As a result, many are already familiar with gourmet foods and actively seek them out.

Skills necessary: You'll need the ability to know what people in your area like when it comes to high-end products, as well as an eye for the next hot food item down the pike.

Investment required: High.

? **For more information:** National Association for the Specialty Food Trade, 120 Wall Street, 27th Floor, New York, NY 10005; 212-482-6440; *www.nasft.org*

Many people decide to open a gourmet food store after they've made it in another business, usually one that has allowed them to sock away a good chunk of money.

And that's a good idea, because it's expensive to open up a specialty food store, first, because it's important for the store to be located in a highly-visible and well-trafficked area, which usually means high rents, and second, because it takes lots of money to develop and create a theme and decor for the shop that fits with the kind of image and message you want to send to customers.

Then, of course, you'll have to fill the shelves. It's impossible to realize that you may have to eat some of your mistakes at first while you test the products that are right for your market. It's okay to experiment a little, but it's better to concentrate on a few niches when you first open your doors, adding new lines after your original stock has proven to be successful. For instance, you may want to focus on specialty foods that are only made in your state. This formula tends to be successful in towns that concentrate on tourist business; visitors always want to take home a little piece of the place they've visited.

Another way to specialize with a gourmet food store is by providing homecooked, ready-made meals to your customer base for take out. As people become even more strapped for time with work and family activities, they'll be looking for more places to purchase tasty, healthy take-out meals to pick up on the way home from work and zap in the microwave for a hassle-free dinner.

Whatever niche you choose, everyone loves good food, but they love it even more when somebody else prepares it and saves them a little bit of time.

48. Graphic Design

 Description of the business: A company that designs printed and online matter for individuals and businesses and coordinates printing and Internet logistics.

 Why it's a good business to start if you don't want to work hard anymore: Today businesses need to have a unifying theme for their corporate image. They also know that it's more cost-effective to farm out graphic design work to a variety of companies rather than keep a designer on staff full time.

 Skills necessary: You'll need an eye for design and layout and professional experience in designing corporate materials. You may also need to employ good sales skills in order to convince a business owner or manager to use your services.

 Investment required: Medium.

 For more information: American Institute of Graphic Arts, 164 Fifth Avenue, New York, NY 10010; 212-807-1990; *www.aiga.org*

We are a visual society, hypnotized and encouraged to buy a certain brand of laundry detergent because of the arrangement of shapes and colors on the box. Most people are unable to explain why they're compelled to

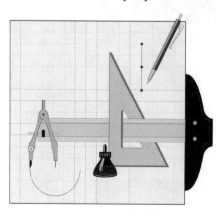

respond to an ad or buy a certain item, even if they need it, except for, "The look got me."

Odds are a professional graphic designer was behind the strategy that turned a staple into an impulse buy. If you'd like to have this kind of influence and you have a good eye for designing striking images that get people to react, opening up a design shop is a good bet. And while having a four-year degree from an art school definitely gives you an edge, the truth is that high-speed computers and sophisticated software programs have made it easy for artistic types to get the work done in a fraction of the time it used to take. You can even be a complete klutz at drawing a straight line. If you can study an ad, brochure, or package and be able to succinctly tell why the way it looks compels people to act, then an intensive course of self-study and lots of practice will go a long way.

49. Handwriting Analysis

 Description of the business: A service that analyzes people's handwriting, which can include lectures and entertainment to social groups and clubs, personality assessment by corporations, compatibility studies, document examination, and vocational guidance.

 Why it's a good business to start if you don't want to work hard anymore: Companies are turning to handwriting analysis more frequently to screen prospective employees, and lawyers are using the science to determine whether a document has been forged. Skilled handwriting analysts are in short supply compared with the demand for their services, and therefore can command high fees.

 Skills necessary: You'll need to complete a formal course of home study in order to become certified as a professional graphologist.

 Investment required: Low.

 For more information: International Graphoanalysis Society, 842 Fifth Avenue, New Kensington, PA 15068; 724-472-9701; *www.igas.com*

People are always fascinated to discover something about themselves that perhaps they didn't know. Likewise, they are interested to find out that some aspect of their personality is confirmed by one of the softer sciences, such as astrology or handwriting analysis.

Yet handwriting analysis is becoming a bona fide screening technique and a way to prove in court if a particular document is legitimate. Some lawyers are even using graphological analysis to select a jury. Frequently, a business will call in a graphologist to analyze the personalities of two or three prospective employees, while attorneys and legal experts rely on handwriting analysts as expert witnesses. One reason why more companies and attorneys are turning to handwriting analysis as a form of psychological assessment is because they can receive results in a matter of hours, while the results from a standardized psychological test may take weeks to arrive.

A handwriting analyst can also serve as an entertainer of sorts, in much the same way as a memory expert, magician, or hypnotist can entertain an audience. More than one handwriting expert has parlayed her skills on a cruise ship vacation, getting free airfare and room and board for a week in exchange for analyzing the handwriting of other guests for about an hour a day.

50. Herb Farming

 Description of the business: An entrepreneur grows herbs to sell in a variety of forms, from potpourri to herbal cosmetics and even loose, in bulk.

 Why it's a good business to start if you don't want to work hard anymore: Today, people are increasingly interested in eating produce that has been grown without chemicals and in using herbal preparations in alternative health practices. Herb farmers with even a short growing season can build a booming business.

 Skills necessary: A green thumb definitely helps, as does a sense for what's popular in the market.

 Investment required: Low.

 For more information: *Herb Quarterly,* 1041 Shary Circle, Concord, CA 94518; 800-371-HERB; *www.herbquarterly.com*

You already know that as life in America gets increasingly high-tech and rushed, more people are yearning for services and products that hint at a simpler time. And as more and more Baby Boomers become AARP members with every passing minute, health issues—and treating them with natural methods—will take front stage for many people.

Herb farming is a kind of business that can be done year-round as well as part-time. Because gardening and growing herbs are already popular hobbies, if you're exploring the possibility of starting an herb farming business, it's a good bet that you already have everything you need to get started. You just have to find your niches and decide how to reach the marketplace.

The good news is that herbal farming is an extremely versatile venture; you can sell the herbs in fresh or dried form, combine them for potpourri mixtures, create garlands or baskets, and prepare herb combinations for cooking. And if you grow a surplus in warmer weather, you can spend your winters drying and packing the herbs or mixing them into a variety of preparations. Some states regulate the types of herbs you can sell on the specialty food market, but there are usually no such restrictions on the sale of fresh herbs or crafts that use herb products.

Other herbalists expand their business to include classes, teaching people how to grow herbs, cook with them, and use them for crafts. Herbal medicine is catching on and will continue to be a fast-growing force in alternative medical practices, and cosmetic preparations made with herbs are also becoming more popular. Even if you live in the frozen North, you can grow herbs indoors year-round with the help of fluorescent lights.

51. Home Healthcare Agency

 Description of the business: A service that places healthcare aides in private homes to assist an elderly or ill person with a variety of tasks.

 Why it's a good business to start if you don't want to work hard anymore: Americans are getting older, living longer, and staying in their own homes as long as they can. Private nurses are expensive, and many housebound people don't need them every day. Health aides are a better choice for many.

 Skills necessary: You'll need to be good at finding and hiring caring workers, and locating the clients who will need them to visit.

 Investment required: Medium.

 For more information: National Association for Home Care and Hospice, 228 Seventh Street SE, Washington, DC 20003; 202-547-7424; *www.nahc.org*

Though it's true that people over the age of 65 need proportionately more medical care than people who are younger, the fact is that, on many of the occasions where a visiting nurse travels to a patient, a home healthcare aide would have fit the bill and cost less to boot.

Home healthcare aides are somewhere in between a housekeeper and a nurse. They provide a variety of personal care services and are frequently called on to shop for groceries and tidy up the house. More importantly, they provide a degree of companionship that elderly housebound men and women find to be the most valuable aspect of the visit.

Home healthcare agencies are responsible for setting appointments with clients and then alerting the aides to their upcoming schedules. The agencies work as a clearinghouse of sorts, hiring competent employees, finding clients in need of their services, and then matching the two of them up on either a sporadic basis or a regular schedule.

The need for good home healthcare agencies will skyrocket beginning in the next few years, given the number of Baby Boomers who are nearing the age of 65.

52. Home Inspection Service

 Description of the business: A service that checks out residential or commercial buildings prior to purchase, in order to point out flaws and categorize the operating systems as sound, to reassure the buyer and the bank or other investor.

 Why it's a good business to start if you don't want to work hard anymore: A nationwide housing boom and an increase in the population and the number of people who are buying homes, either for the first time or to trade up, translates into a business that will be in demand for the foreseeable future.

 Skills necessary: You'll need a thorough knowledge of the inner workings of a home and its various systems, as well as a detective's eye to look for clues that point to potential problems in the structure.

 Investment required: Low.

 For more information: American Society of Home Inspectors, 932 Lee Street, Suite 101, Des Plaines, IL 60016; 847-759-2820; *www.ashi.com*

Everyone dreams of owning their own home. If you are already a home-owner, then you probably dream of buying another home that is a step up from your current residence. Regardless of the type of house you desire, the chances are good that, before you buy, you'll want to hire a professional home inspector to go over the house with an analytical eye, to point out potential problems and to reassure you about others.

If you think you'd like to be able to do this kind of work for a business, you should know that in many areas the field is wide open when it comes to competent home inspectors. In most states, it's not necessary to be licensed or to possess a minimum level of education. However, if you want to become certified by the American Society of Home Inspectors—and therefore considered to be a rung above noncertified inspectors in the  eyes of real estate agents—you'll need to first pass a test. Once you're a member, the realtors from whom you'll derive the great majority of business referrals will feel comfortable recommending that their clients hire you for your services.

In any case, if you enjoy seeing a variety of homes and can provide an accurate and unbiased report on the general condition of the house, you'll love running a home inspection business.

53. Homeschooling Consulting

 Description of the business: An entrepreneur works with parents who homeschool their children to make sure they're satisfying basic education requirements that are set by their state educational board.

 Why it's a good business to start if you don't want to work hard anymore: Homeschooling is on the increase, as more and more local and state school boards accept it as another way kids can get a good education.

 Skills necessary: You'll need a background in education— preferably a resume that includes at least one teaching appointment—and the ability to feel comfortable dealing with parents and state bureaucracy.

 Investment required: Low.

 For more information: Family Learning Organization, PO Box 7247, Spokane, WA 99207; 509-467-2552; *www.familylearning.org*

It's not news that more parents are becoming dissatisfied with the quality of education their children are receiving in public schools. What is news is that home schooling, once scorned by the state and school boards, is becoming a widely accepted and even preferable method of education.

Some school boards still put parents who want to teach their children at home through the wringer, but the majority just want to see that parents can provide a balanced curriculum for their kids and that they have sufficient interest and time to teach them at home. The majority of parents need some guidance on structuring lesson plans and activities that will please the state and nurture their kids. Many are turning to homeschooling experts to help them, primarily before they make the initial foray, but also to occasionally check in with them to make sure they're on the right track and they're not shortchanging their kids.

If this sounds like a good business for you, it's a wide open field. Though it's possible to find clients online, the fact is that you'll probably be able to find potential clients more easily in rural areas than in suburbs or cities, where both parents tend to work full-time. You may also have to learn the customs of individual state educational agencies, but at least you, your clients, the agencies, and local school boards are all on the same side, wanting children to have the best education they can.

54. House-sitting Agency

 Description of the business: A service that hires independent contractors to house-sit for clients.

 Why it's a good business to start if you don't want to work hard anymore: More people are traveling more frequently and for shorter periods of time, but they don't want their homes to be unprotected. Running an agency that matches up house sitters with homeowners provides a much-needed service. And you'll have the contractors doing the lion's share of work for you.

 Skills necessary: You should enjoy juggling many tasks at once and like to work with a variety of people.

 Investment required: Low.

 For more information: Home Sitters on Wheels of America, 5200 Torrey Pines Court, Carmichael, CA 95808; 916-973-8850; *www.homesitters.net*

Running a house-sitting agency is very much like running an employment agency, except it's more relaxed. A successful agency in an urban area can easily have up to 100 sitters on call—among them, students, freelance writers, and senior citizens—and book up to 750 sitter days each month. The average length of time a sitter will stay on each job is seven to 10 days. Usually, the daily fee is split 50/50 between the agency and the sitter.

A house-sitting agency is an easy business to start and run from home because, aside from the initial interview and client visit, the primary contact you'll have with both homeowners and sitters will be over the phone. A first visit to a homeowner's residence will involve lots of note-taking, roughly-drawn maps, and many questions about the necessary chores, duties, and expectations of a sitter. The first interview with a potential house sitter occurs once the sitter has filled out an application and provided details on personal habits, such as smoking, driving ability, and allergies. Then after all references have been thoroughly checked, along with a credit report, the agency owner meets the prospective sitter.

Aside from ads in local papers and the Yellow Pages, the majority of house-sitting clients come as repeat business and referrals from satisfied customers. House-sitting is definitely a service that will be more in demand in the coming years.

55. Human Resources Consulting

 Description of the business: A company that serves as the personnel department for other businesses, from passing out tax forms to interviewing to training new employees to calculating benefits plans.

 Why it's a good business to start if you don't want to work hard anymore: With more microbusinesses appearing on the horizon (companies with fewer than 10 employees), most of these enterprises can't afford to hire a full-time human resources person. A consultant works part-time, doesn't take up room in the office, and is exposed to a variety of businesses for a wealth of business experience.

 Skills necessary: Previous experience in human relations is necessary. The ability to find new employees and deal with problem workers is also vital.

 Investment required: Medium.

For more information: National Human Resources Association, PO Box 803, Pewaukee, WI 53072; 866-523-4417; *www.humanresources.org*

It's often said that information is the new currency for the 21st century, but the truth is it's the people who will help to create the information and then broadcast it to the world.

People are vital to any business, whether they're clients or employees. But while the majority of new enterprises may take on several employees from the start, business owners don't have the time to handle personnel issues. Besides, few of them need to retain a full-time human resources expert on staff.

An HR consultant can perform a number of duties, from placing help-wanted ads, screening resumes, and doing the initial interviews, to shopping for benefits plans and handling employee complaints, or just consulting with a business owner for a set period of time about the number and types of employees she'll need to hire that will best suit her business. Some HR consultants specialize in a particular industry, though personnel skills can be transferred to just about any field. If you have a background in personnel and have always dreamed of going out on your own, the timing couldn't be better for your venture, given the number of entrepreneurs, in all industries, who will be eager to make use of your services.

56. Import Business

 Description of the business: A business that specializes in bringing products to the United States from overseas and selling them to wholesale and/or retail markets.

 Why it's a good business to start if you don't want to work hard anymore: As more people travel overseas as a matter of course, they become more familiar with products from foreign countries and more amenable to purchasing them on American shores.

 Skills necessary: You'll need stellar negotiation skills, proficiency in at least one other language, and the ability to go with the flow when dealing with cultures different from yours.

 Investment required: Medium.

 For more information: *Import/Export: How to Get Started in International Trade*, by Carl A. Nelson (McGraw-Hill, 2000).

If you love to travel and would love to get paid for it, then running an import business is the way to go, but a word of warning: It helps to be the adventurous type.

One example of an import business is to buy handmade woolen goods from South America, such as sweaters, caps, mittens, scarves, and wall hangings, and then bring them back to sell to stores, wholesalers, distributors, or even directly to consumers via a mail-order catalog or Website. In reality, you can import virtually any product, but experienced importers say that in order to be successful in this business, you'll need to specialize in a particular item or ethnic group, offering unique products that are not readily available in this country. Even then, there are no guarantees, as the import business can sometimes amount to a crapshoot of sorts, because consumer tastes are fickle, and an item that sold quickly a month ago may just collect dust a few weeks later.

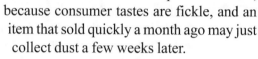

If you don't like wrestling with a load of red tape, you should pick another business, because importers must deal not only with U.S. customs, paying fees as well as freight home, but the government of the country from which you're exporting will want to exact its pound of flesh as well. Savvy importers hire an agent on the American side to do all the paperwork and herd the items through customs with the least hassle possible.

Needless to say, importers who are familiar with the culture and language of the country where they're purchasing their goods will thrive more than someone who is disrespectful of the social protocol of the culture.

57. Information Brokering

Description of the business: A service that collects information for another business or an individual and provides it in a form the client is able to use.

Why it's a good business to start if you don't want to work hard anymore: Although information is everywhere, few people know exactly where to look for it and put it into a report that's easily accessible to the end user. There's a great need for the human bloodhounds who can ferret out this information.

Skills necessary: Computer proficiency is mandatory, along with a sixth sense of where to locate the information. You'll need the ability to translate the information into a report in plain English.

Investment required: Medium.

For more information: *Sawyer's Survival Guide for Information Brokers*, by Deborah C. Sawyer (Information Plus, Inc., 1995). or contact:
Burwell Enterprises, 5619 Plumtree Drive, Dallas, TX 75252; 972-732-0160; *www.burwellinc.com*

"Get me copy!" used to be a common refrain in the newspaper business. The war cry today, in businesses everywhere, is "Get me information!" Corporations, independent professionals, and even creative artists rely on certain pieces of information to help them get their jobs done—not to mention to make them look good to their own clients.

But no one has the time to look for the information they need, which may be buried deep in a government Website or in the archives of an obscure news journal. Even if they had the time, not everyone is skilled enough to know where to look.

Starting a business as an information broker is a very wise move for the 21st century. Because people have been complaining about information overload since the 1990s, you can expect that it's just going to get worse. After all, the flow of information certainly isn't going to slow down. Consultants, attorneys, and corporations will probably be the best market for your services. In fact, anyone who runs his own business offering a professional service to clients will be your most likely candidate.

You may be asked to dig for census figures, find county records from a century ago, or report on how many black Trans Ams were produced in 1993, but if you have a stubborn streak and are perennially curious, becoming a broker of information will be a good choice for you.

58. Intellectual Property Consulting

 Description of the business: An entrepreneur counsels businesses and individuals who work with information to help determine how to package, sell, and protect it.

 Why it's a good business to start if you don't want to work hard anymore: With the technology explosion, information is the new currency in the business world, whether it's managing it or circulating it. However, few people are familiar with the various rights and legal issues surrounding information.

 Skills necessary: It's ideal if you have a legal background, preferably as an attorney, although people with publishing experience specializing in rights and permissions will be able to tackle many jobs.

 Investment required: Medium.

For more information: American Intellectual Property Law Association, 2001 Jefferson Davis Highway, Suite 203, Arlington, VA 22202; 703-415-0780; *www.aipla.org*

Like it or not, corporate America has finally made the switch from being a manufacturing society to an information society. Information is more valuable than gold in some arenas, and this means that entire industries have sprung up where they didn't even exist five years ago.

One rapidly growing industry involves the management of all this information. An intellectual property consultant is able to put a value on a particular piece of information, locate the market for it, and know how to reach consumers and what to charge for it, all the while not losing control of it completely.

An intellectual property consultant's services may range from advising an individual how to protect his idea or information product to counseling a software company on how to structure a royalty deal with a programmer, who owns the rights to the work, and how to license the work internationally.

Intellectual property consulting will become more challenging as more media are invented, which, these days, occurs about once a week. Shrewd bargaining skills combined with a view for the demand for a product and/or idea, not only today but a year or more down the road, will come in handy should you decide to become a consultant on intellectual property.

59. Internet Consulting

 Description of the business: A service that advises businesses and executives on the best ways to use the Internet to promote their ventures and conduct online research.

 Why it's a good business to start if you don't want to work hard anymore: Many people still view the Internet as the modern-day equivalent of the wild west and will gladly pay someone else to guide them through the maze of research or where to find a competent Web page designer.

 Skills necessary: A familiarity with the Internet and its applications for business, as well as a nose for what's on the horizon.

 Investment required: Medium.

 For more information: *How to Be a Successful Internet Consultant,* by Jessica Keyes (Amacom, 1996).

For those of us who live online, it's hard to imagine that most people feel intimidated by the vast reaches of the Web and that businesses are not aware of the advantages of conducting commerce and doing research online.

Starting a business as an Internet consultant will allow you to work with businesses of all shapes and sizes, in order to help them learn one of two things: how employees can efficiently navigate the Web and the numerous methods that exist for businesses to promote themselves online.

In a way, an Internet consultant serves as a conductor of sorts, leading employees in a joyous cacophony of noise online as you help them to serve their own unique needs. If you love to spend hours online and prefer to stay involved in a number of different ventures, becoming an Internet consultant is your best bet.

If, however, you choose to specialize in a particular aspect of Internet work, as it pertains to businesses, one of the other Internet businesses included in this book—from Website designer to e-commerce consultant—would be an ideal venue in which to focus your skills and attention.

When it comes to the Internet, the one rule is that change happens faster than Quick Draw McGraw, so while you work in one area today, always be on the lookout for the next big trend.

60. Landscaping

 Description of the business: A service that maintains and/or plans and designs a lawn or garden for residences or businesses.

 Why it's a good business to start if you don't want to work hard anymore: Taking care of the grounds around a home or office can be very time-consuming. Most people don't have the time, but they still want to have a healthy, attractive landscape, and they're willing to pay for it. Depending upon where you live, this can be a business that allows you to take up to half the year off.

 Skills necessary: Obviously, a green thumb helps, along with an eye for being able to visualize the completed lay of the land before you pick up a shovel.

 Investment required: Medium.

 For more information: Associated Landscape Contractors of America, 150 Elden Street, Suite 270, Herndon, VA 20170; 800-395-ALCA; *www.alca.org*

People love their lawns, whether they're at home or work. Even a small patch in the middle of an otherwise concrete jungle makes a big difference in the attitude of the people who pass it by. But a lush green lawn is not simply created; it's carefully planned, tended, and nurtured along every step of the way. It's a labor-intensive process that has most people reluctant to spend the little time they have. Enter the landscape technician, whose job it is to help a client's lawn look like the lawn of their dreams. If you're interested in pursuing landscape work as your own business, you should know that it's much more than pushing a lawnmower, and that it tends to be a full-time seasonal job, which can free up your winters for other pursuits, business or leisure.

Despite the proliferation of franchised landscape companies, many homeowners still prefer to hire a locally-owned company. While there may be a good amount of competition in your area, all it takes is one look at the number of lawns in town that need regular maintenance, and you should realize that you'll have your hands full for at least six months out of the year, even in the northernmost parts of the United States.

A landscape technician needn't be limited to lawns, however; many also specialize in a particular niche, working on golf courses, groundskeeping at public buildings (including schools), or even choosing to just fertilize a lawn. Although a landscape technician can become certified by the Associated Landscape Contractors of America, most homeowners and businesses only require that you know your stuff well enough to do a neat, clean job.

61. Mailing List Consulting

 Description of the business: A consultant advises individuals and businesses on the best type of postal or electronic mailing list to rent or buy. A consultant may also be competent in writing and designing direct-mail pieces.

 Why it's a good business to start if you don't want to work hard anymore: As more companies discover direct mail to be an effective way to reach customers, they'll need more targeted mailing lists to find them.

 Skills necessary: A marketing background helps. You'll need to discern the best possible market for the product or service promoted in the mailing and be able to project the demographics from a particular list onto the people who are most likely to respond to the mailing.

 Investment required: Medium.

 For more information: Direct Marketing Association, 1120 Avenue of the Americas, New York, NY 10036; 212-768-7277; *www.the-dma-org*

Although everyone gripes about receiving too many solicitations through the mail, the truth is that if it didn't work, companies wouldn't be sending out billions of pieces of mail every year.

The direct-mail industry is taking the same approach as other marketing industries and breaking down their targeted audiences into niche categories that become smaller but more specific. In this way, a mailing list consultant can help a magazine for women rock climbers, for instance, know that their direct mail package will bring in more subscribers by not only renting a mailing list from a company that sells shoes specifically for rock climbers, but by narrowing it down to only the women's names that appear on the list.

Many businesspeople aren't aware that marketing has become this targeted, and even if they are, many don't know where to go to locate the specialized mailing lists they'll need. That's where a mailing list consultant comes in. There are hundreds of different agencies that rent out specific mailing lists, but many handle only general lists, with industries broken down by SIC (Standard Industrial Classification) code and geographic location, or by regular customers of a specialty catalog who've spent more than a certain amount in a particular year.

While these lists may work for a direct mailing, a consultant will be familiar with breaking the desired audience down into even smaller but more accurate categories and have ideas for testing a smaller portion of the list before expanding the mailing to the entire list.

If, as a mailing list consultant, you can save your clients money, while pulling in stellar results, they'll be likely to use your services again.

62. Masonry

Description of the business: A service where workers lay stone to build walls and floors, and construct fireplaces and chimneys with bricks and concrete blocks.

Why it's a good business to start if you don't want to work hard anymore: More people are demanding handcrafted stonework in their houses, on their patios, and on stone walls and hearths in their yards. There aren't enough masons to handle all the work that's out there, which results in a high hourly rate, along with the ability to pick and choose your jobs.

Skills necessary: Physical strength and endurance, and an exacting eye for placement and detail. An apprenticeship is usually served before going out on your own.

Investment required: Low.

For more information: International Union of Bricklayers and Allied Craftsmen, 1776 Eye Street NW, Washington, DC 20006; 202-783-3788; *www.bacweb.org*

If you are looking to start a business where you can exercise your creativity and you also are as strong as an ox, a mason relies on both every day. You'll probably never get bored, because the variety of jobs a mason is called upon to do is expansive: A mason will build a walkway, construct a chimney and hearth—indoors or out—lay marble flooring, build an historically accurate stone wall that crisscrosses an estate, and build retaining walls to prevent a hillside from collapsing into 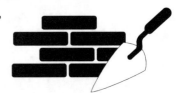 the roadway. Masons will also need to know how to repair cracks and imperfections in existing stone and masonry work in order to prolong a structure's life.

Laying stone is probably one of the most physically demanding business there is, but one of the most satisfying. Many masons start out by enrolling in an apprenticeship program sponsored by a local chapter of the International Union of Bricklayers and Allied Craftsmen. A typical apprenticeship consists of three years of full-time training on the job, along with 144 hours of classroom time spent learning safety issues and how to read blueprints and design basic layouts.

Once training is complete, a mason can pick a specialty. One rapidly growing area in regions with a supply of houses built with stone and/or brick, is the restoration of homes that are beginning to show their age. Others include decorative masonry work in home interiors and a specialization in laying stone for office buildings and other public construction. Because the work is so difficult, few kids are choosing the field after high school, and so it's likely that even in times when the economy stumbles, a skilled mason should have more work than he can handle.

63. Massage Therapy

 Description of the business: A specialist offers massage to individuals, either working in conjunction with other health-related businesses and/or through a private practice.

 Why it's a good business to start if you don't want to work hard anymore: People are working harder and longer, and their bodies are showing the stress. Alternative medical practices—including massage therapy—are increasingly being recommended by traditional medical experts as a healthy way to heal the body. Plus, the hourly rate can be quite high, especially in urban areas.

 Skills necessary: In most states, you'll need to attend a certified massage school and take a minimum number of class hours. After study is completed, you'll most likely need to take an examination in order to become licensed by the state.

 Investment required: Medium.

 For more information: American Massage Therapy Association, 820 Davis Street, Suite 100, Evanston, IL 60201; 847-864-0123; *www.amtamassage.org*

More than a few people who have become massage therapists have entered the field because of the effect that massage therapy had on their own physical and emotional well-being. Not long ago, any kind of body-work treatments—from chiropractic to massage therapy—was viewed by the traditional medical establishment as nothing more than quackery. Today, of course, as laypersons and medical practitioners wake up to the benefits of bodywork techniques, demand for massage therapists is increasing.

Most therapists start their practice by setting up shop at a health club or with a medical specialist, such as a physical therapist or chiropractor. In this way, you can build up your own roster of clients so that when you go out on your own you'll have a built-in client base. Plus, the skills are extremely mobile, so if you decide you'd like to move to another part of the country, chances are you can be up and running as a self-employed therapist within the constructs of a medically-oriented business in a new area within a few weeks.

Here's something else to keep in mind: If you have a tendency towards overwork, massage therapy is one of the few businesses listed in this book where it's impossible to work around the clock; your body simply won't be able to take it.

64. Medical Claims Processing

 Description of the business: A service that takes complete charge of a medical practice's insurance billing systems, from filing a claim electronically to keeping track of the deposits.

 Why it's a good business to start if you don't want to work hard anymore: As HMOs consume an ever-greater percentage of America's medical practices, it's not cost-effective for a doctor's office to handle medical claims in-house, there's just too much paperwork. You can run this business from a home computer, and subcontract to others so that you make money while they work as well.

 Skills necessary: You should be comfortable working with computers and serving as the liaison between physician or dentist and the insurance company.

 Investment required: Medium.

 For more information: *Start Your Own Medical Claims and Transcription Business* (Prentice Hall, 1999).

Although physicians and dentists are required to keep up with the latest in medical studies and high-tech diagnostic equipment for their practices, they often tend to lag behind when it comes to the latest method of processing claims to send to insurance companies. Currently, only about a quarter of all insurance claims are processed electronically, at a cost of about $1.10 per claim to the insurance company. Processing a traditional paper claim costs between $7.50 and $20, which is one reason why insurance rates are so high, as companies are forced to pass the cost along to consumers and physicians.

Not only does electronic processing cost less, but the turnaround time is shorter. Traditional payment time to the doctor can take from 30 to 90 days after the insurance company receives the claim. With electronic processing, a medical practice will typically receive a check for payment— electronically deposited, of course, within two weeks.

But it takes a lot of time for a medical staff to learn the process and how to use the necessary software. Besides that, a practice would need to invest in the software—a cost which can be substantial. This is why an increasing number of medical practices are outsourcing their claims processing work. This business will only grow in demand as the government agencies responsible for Medicare and Medicaid mandates require the medical practitioners who work with them to file all claims electronically and agree to receive payment in the same fashion. Look for other insurance companies to follow suit, and the demand for medical claims processing services to continue.

65. Medical Transcribing

 Description of the business: A service that converts a physician's notes and/or tape recordings into hard copy and disks for patients' records for future reference.

 Why it's a good business to start if you don't want to work hard anymore: Physician's handwriting has always been lousy, but medical malpractice insurance companies are demanding that physicians keep accurate, detailed records, forcing them to outsource transcription work to agencies.

 Skills necessary: You'll need to be familiar with medical terminology and be a quick, accurate typist.

 Investment required: Medium.

? **For more information:** The Medical Transcription Industry Alliance, 77 Broadway East, Seattle, WA 98102; 800-543-MTIA; *www.mtia.com*

Time-pressed physicians are often forced to jot down notes or to speak medical jargon into a tape recorder in order to keep track of a patient's condition, diagnosis, and subsequent treatment. Once upon a time, many medical practices had the luxury of keeping at least one full-time transcriptionist on staff, but as more physicians and office managers are forced to cut down on overhead, as a result of reduced payments from HMOs, Medicare, and other health agencies, they've begun to look for other options.

They still need to have taped notes and pages of scrawled data tran-scribed to add to a patient's record, but instead of paying for a staff transcriptionist's downtime, more medical practices are starting to farm out the work to an agency. This is especially vital because the Institute of Medicine in Washington has dictated that a standardized patient record system be the format every physician follows, in order to facilitate the entry and extraction of crucial patient information. This means that those physicians who have been postponing the inevitable are going to have to invest in a full-time transcriptionist—an unlikely scenario due to HMO limits on office overhead expenses, as well as the extra space requirements—or take the easiest and most painless course, and outsource all transcription work.

66. Mobile Beauty Service

 Description of the business: A hairdresser and/or an esthetician travels to her customers to cut and style their hair and perform other beauty services.

 Why it's a good business to start if you don't want to work hard anymore: People have to have their hair cut and even colored or permed on a regular basis, but scheduling appointments can sometimes be impossible. If their beautician comes to them, they're much less likely to break an appointment. You can pick and choose your schedule and charge higher rates than if you had a station in a shop.

 Skills necessary: You should already have experience and a beautician's license in your state, and a loyal following.

 Investment required: Low.

 For more information: Contact a local beauty school.

While some people might view a housecall from their beautician as the ultimate luxury, many others might quickly come to regard it as a necessity, after experiencing it just once. Many service busi-nesses have gone mobile in recent years, including car detailers, but applying the concept to the idea of getting your hair cut and styled in the comfort and privacy of your home or even office, well, this is a small price for many people to pay. In addition to offering hair care, you may even wish to broaden your business by offering cosmetology and manicure services. Because you'll need to be working in the field already to become a mobile beautician, if you're considering expanding your business to incorporate regular house visits, you can start by asking your regular customers if they'd prefer to have you come to them, instead of vice versa. Many will probably jump at the chance.

The good news is that many mobile beauticians end up making more money by being on the road than in a shop, because overhead is virtually nonexistent and many people will actually pay a premium for the housecall. Many beauticians choose to combine the two and have a storefront and also offer the mobile services, but I'd bet that most, if not all, of your customers would rather see you on their own turf than have to slog through traffic to get to yours.

67. Monthly Mail-order Club

 Description of the business: A business where customers subscribe in order to receive a product every month—or less often—that follows a theme, such as cigar of the month or coffee of the month.

 Why it's a good business to start if you don't want to work hard anymore: People are buying more items through the mail, but they like to be introduced to items they wouldn't be able to find out about on their own. Signing up with a monthly mail-order club allows them to do just that.

 Skills necessary: You'll need to know where to go to get unusual and hard-to-find items and be able to market the club effectively.

 Investment required: Low.

 For more information: *How to Start a Home-Based Mail Order Business,* by Georganne Fiumara (Globe Pequot Press, 1999).

People love surprises, and when those surprises arrive in the mailbox, it can seem a little bit like Christmas. Monthly mail-order clubs have been around for decades, most popularly, the various monthly fruit and book clubs. However, the sky's the limit when it comes to the variety of items that can be ordered through a subscription-based venture; we've seen condom of the month, chocolate of the month, even cat toy of the month.

If this sounds like it's right up your alley, you should think of a hobby or leisure activity in which you participate on a regular basis. What kind of product would *you* like to receive in the mail once a month that could both help you improve this activity and would expose you to a number of different items that would be difficult to locate on your own, even if you had the time?

Chances are that if you're interested in it, there are other people participating in the same activity who would love to receive a new item in the mail every month. Once you decide on your focus, you can reach your target audience with a Website and with press releases sent to the publications and other media that cover your activity. It's a good idea to offer a variety of membership plans to subscribers, from an item every month to a sampler plan, in which a customer can try out your service for three months.

The great thing about a mail-order club is that it can be run in your spare time in the beginning, and it may lead to a much larger business, in time, as you decide to sell other items in the same category to your list of existing customers. It's a great first stepping-stone to a sizable empire.

68. Multimedia Production

 Description of the business: A business that uses word processing, graphics, and audio and video software to create multimedia CDs and packages for businesses to use to promote their own products and services.

 Why it's a good business to start if you don't want to work hard anymore: Just as many video games and Web pages have turned into movies in miniature, in order to capture the attention of an audience, information producers in other industries need to ramp up the entertainment quotient of their products as well.

 Skills necessary: You should have a familiarity with graphics design, as well as audio and video software, and also have scriptwriting talents, or at least be able to tell a story that's entertaining, complete, and compelling.

 Investment required: Medium.

 For more information: Software & Information Industry Association, 1090 Vermont Avenue NW, Sixth Floor, Washington, DC 20005; 202-289-7442; *www.siia.net*

If you've always been a frustrated movie producer and you love to work with computers and design Web pages or graphic pieces, you may think that the field of multimedia production is the answer to your prayers. The good news is that you don't have to kowtow to Hollywood bigwigs in order to have all the work you want.

Although there are a number of different markets a multimedia producer can pursue, by far, the largest and most lucrative consist of businesses that want to jazz up their image and presentations for both clients and the general public. Businesses require multimedia to replace the now old-fashioned materials such as training videos, video and traditional press releases, audio tapes and videos to motivate an internal sales force, even informational CDs used by human resources departments to persuade potential employees to join the company.

If you are comfortable working with a broad base of software and hardware, ultimedia equipment isn't hard to tackle. Plus, as the equipment gets easier to use and cheaper to buy with each passing month, it will cost you less to have the up-to-the-minute equipment and software necessary to make your multimedia business a roaring success.

69. Niche Marketing Agency

 Description of the business: A marketing service that offers advice to businesses and entrepreneurs whose products and services are aimed at audiences that are small and sometimes difficult to reach.

 Why it's a good business to start if you don't want to work hard anymore: Generalist marketing—a la *Reader's Digest* and the evening news—is not only very expensive but it's virtually extinct. Marketers realize that going after a smaller, very targeted group of customers will reap much better results. Develop a specialty in a valuable field and you can pretty much call the shots.

 Skills necessary: You should have a background in marketing and excel at ferreting out tiny segments of the population, whether business-related or consumer. It's also necessary to be comfortable integrating many different kinds of marketing into one unified marketing plan.

 Investment required: Medium.

 For more information: American Marketing Association, 311 S. Wacker Drive, Chicago, IL 60606; 312-542-9000; *www.marketingpower.com*

We have become a nation of tens of thousands of special interest groups, each with its own magazine, association, convention, Internet mailing list—you name it. And no matter how obscure the interest and narrow the focus, a company with a product or service to sell to these groups will be able to reach their niche audience.

Because many of these microcompanies were started by people for whom the primary focuses of the businesses were hobbies, the founders may not be skilled when it comes to marketing, and they'll be able to use your services. If you decide to become a niche marketing consultant, you should know that you'll be able to specialize as well, whether it's advising small companies that sell to women executives, for example, or focusing on companies in different fields that all market their wares to small, select audiences.

Although it may be easy to find all the various forums and publications that cater to niche audiences, it's important that you can sense the most appropriate way to send a message to that market. Clearly, aficionados in any category will be turned off by a message that is created by someone who's not familiar with their passion. In other words, the ability to play a chameleon helps, as does being empathetic. Marketing to niche audiences will exercise your creativity like no other kind of marketing.

70. Old House Restoration

 Description of the business: A business where a skilled contractor or tradesman buys and repairs a house specifically to rent or sell after it's fixed-up.

 Why it's a good business to start if you don't want to work hard anymore: Older homes will continue to be in demand among people who appreciate the craftsmanship of the past.

 Skills necessary: You'll need some expertise with carpentry and other restorative techniques, as well as a good eye for the diamonds in the rough. Negotiation skills also help when dealing with subcontractors, real estate agents, and government agencies.

 Investment required: Medium.

? **For more information:** *Renovating and Restyling Older Homes,* by Lawrence Dworin (Craftsman Book Company, 1996).

It's one of the most popular continuing American dreams: buy a beat-up old house, fix it up, and sell it at a significant profit. With the population growing and some towns stretched to the limit as far as developable land, fixing up an old house will be the only way to enter a tight housing market with little money, or to make a profit buying and selling real estate.

Beware: Buying, fixing, and selling an old house is not as easy as it looks. But if you have a little cash, you'll have a lot of bargaining power when dealing with sellers, particularly banks and mortgage companies that are foreclosing on questionable properties.

The first key is to look for buildings that aren't falling into the ground. Residential buildings that need cosmetic work and require perhaps a bit of structural work to get them into shape are preferable. If the building has been on the market awhile, so much the better.

It's a good idea to concentrate on reasonable neighborhoods—up-and-coming areas are always a good idea—and you should know when to contract out the work that would be difficult for you to handle by yourself, such as Sheetrock installation. As well, while you may feel capable of doing a lot of the work in an old home on your own, it's essential to contract out some types of work, such as plumbing and electrical, to licensed professionals so that you meet local codes and so the home will pass inspection.

Restoring an old home is a good bet if you love working on old houses, don't mind the hard work, and are able to let it go when you're done.

71. Outplacement Consulting

 Description of the business: A consultant assists corporations and individuals by helping departing employees find new employment and learn how to emotionally deal with leaving the company.

 Why it's a good business to start if you don't want to work hard anymore: Corporations will not only need to outsource the standard outplacement services they offer, but as more companies merge and become acquired, a number of departments will be rendered obsolete, making more employees eligible for outplacement.

 Skills necessary: A background in human resources and/or counseling is important; it's also a good idea to be familiar with companies in the region that might make good potential employers for the clients you'll work with.

 Investment required: Low.

 For more information: International Association of Career Consulting Firms, 1910 Cochran Road, Manor Oak Two, Suite 740, Pittsburgh, PA 15220; 800-565-2182; *www.iaccf.com*

Regardless of the state of the job market, people in all industries will still be looking for jobs, whether to get promoted, to transfer to a particular company, or to move to another region of the country.

An outplacement consultant will be able to help find employment, whether working directly with the employee or contracting with the company letting the employee go. An increasing number of companies work with outside consultants to help place employees in other jobs when the displacement is caused by the company, and not due to the performance of the employee.

Obviously, a vast network of contacts at a number of corporations and businesses helps, and outplacement consultants tend to specialize in a particular field in order to streamline placement opportunities. Some, however, work as generalists, maintaining contacts in a wide variety of fields, which can go a long way toward helping people use the opportunity of losing a job as a chance to branch out into an entirely new field.

72. Pack and Ship Service

Description of the business: A business that offers mailing and package services and personal mailboxes to individuals and businesses from a storefront location.

Why it's a good business to start if you don't want to work hard anymore: People are increasingly prizing convenience over economy, and will often opt to pay a little bit more at a shop nearby that will wrap and ship their packages for them. The more services and options you offer, as long as you in turn contract them out or hire people to handle it for you, the better.

Skills necessary: You'll need to have good rapport with people, deal with the logistics of preparing shipments, and market the business.

Investment required: Medium to high.

For more information: Mail Boxes Etc., 6060 Cornerstone Court West, San Diego, CA 92121; 877-462-3622; *www.mbe.com*

Sometimes it seems that the best businesses to start are those that promise to do it all for their customers, while providing competent and highly personalized service.

A pack and ship service is a great example of this kind of venture. Pack and ship stores offer a variety of services under one roof, and they're usually open for longer hours than their competitors, including the post office and private shipping companies.

A pack and ship business would fit right into a busy neighborhood with a number of other convenience-oriented businesses nearby. For instance, pack-and-ships are frequently located in strip malls and are either adjacent or on the way to other stores and businesses that people need to visit on a regular basis, such as a bakery, supermarket, even a newsstand. While other delivery service drop-off spots may be a few miles away, people who find pack and ship stores tucked in between businesses they frequent more, are likely to use their services, including wrapping their package—even if it costs them more.

Pack and ship stores often respond to consumer demand, offering additional services on an as-needed basis, which can include film processing and Internet access. If you choose to open a pack and ship service, don't be surprised if you end up providing many more services to your customers than just wrapping and shipping packages for them.

73. Painting

 Description of the business: A business specializing in painting building exteriors and/or rooms in homes and offices.

 Why it's a good business to start if you don't want to work hard anymore: The insides and outsides of houses and offices need to be painted on a regular basis. While homeowners, in particular, may have done it themselves every few years, most people are busier today than they were even several years ago. Schedule the bulk of your work in the summer, when you can hire college students, and you'll have a seasonal business that generates great revenue.

 Skills necessary: You should obviously like to paint, have an attention to detail, and be able to deal with all kinds of people.

 Investment required: Low.

? **For more information:** *Painting Contractor: Start and Run a Money-Making Business,* by Dan Ramsey and Walter Curtis (McGraw-Hill/TAB Electronics, 1993).

Many a college student has paid his or her yearly tuition by painting houses. And while some may have not been particularly fond of the activity, it served a purpose and there was probably more work available than there were college students to do it all.

If you were one of the few who actually enjoyed painting houses and interior walls, you'll probably never starve if you decide to start a business painting the interiors and exteriors of houses and office buildings. While the majority of homeowners and office building owners think of having their structures painted in the warm-weather months, many painters are able to keep a busy schedule year-round by painting interiors in the fall and winter, or by branching out into offering wallpaper services as well.

If you cringe at the thought of wielding a brush and paint can on top of a ladder, you should know the high-tech revolution has made even the job of painting easier and faster. Powerful pressure washers and paint sprayers make it possible to perform tasks of cleaning and painting the outside of a house in less than a day. The prep work of taping windows and painting trim will actually consume more time.

The good news is that the prices many painters charge to do an entire house haven't come down, even though the job can be done in a fraction of the time it used to take. By itself, this may give you second thoughts about the validity of painting houses as a business venture, especially if you like to spend your days outdoors and active. After all, this isn't your father's paint anymore.

74. Personal Chef

 Description of the business: An experienced cook travels to a client's home or office to prepare one dinner or enough frozen meals to last several weeks.

 Why it's a good business to start if you don't want to work hard anymore: While many people are concerned with the nutritional value of the foods they eat, most don't have the time to spend preparing it. Having a cook prepare enough meals for a week or two in their own home is worth the added expense for many people.

 Skills necessary: Experience spent in a restaurant is preferable, but naturally talented cooks will be able to find work.

 Investment required: Low.

 For more information: United States Personal Chef Association, 481 Rio Rancho Boulevard NE, Rio Rancho, NM 87124; 800-995-2138; *www.uspca.com*

More than half of every dollar Americans spend on food goes to pay for meals prepared by others. Although most of that amount is spent on restaurant meals and take-out food, a growing percentage is paying for personal chefs. These freelance cooks have regular clients they cook for, whether it's a relaxing candlelight dinner for two, or 10 different casseroles that can be frozen ahead of time and microwaved when needed.

Americans have harried lives, and with outside activities claiming more leisure time than ever before, people just don't have the time—or desire—to cook a meal from scratch. But dining out every night gets expensive and eating fast food and frozen dinners gets old fast. Having a personal chef prepare homemade meals in advance is a boon to busy people who like to eat well at home but don't have the time or desire to cook.

The outlook for personal chefs is bright, especially in metropolitan areas where a majority of households contain two full-time working professionals with children. A personal chef basically plans the menus, shops for the groceries and prepares the meals, usually at the client's home, using the equipment already there.

Although people without restaurant experience can become personal chefs, seasoned culinary professionals who are burned out from working long hours in restaurants or spending weekends catering special events are also attracted to the business for the flexibility and chance to create new menus and recipes every day. Because many clients have dietary restrictions, recipes will often need to be customized.

If you are a talented cook and like the challenge of preparing different menus every day, you can build a thriving business in short order.

75. Personal Financial Planning

 Description of the business: An entrepreneur advises individuals about financial issues, including tax preparation, long-term savings plans, insurance, stock sales, and estate planning.

 Why it's a good business to start if you don't want to work hard anymore: The sheer amount of investment and financial information that exists today is overwhelming. Most people don't have the time or desire to dig through the myriad of options, and would like to have a professional financial expert they can discuss their choices with. Lately, they are more likely to pay a fee to a financial planner than to work with a planner who only makes money off the commissions from products he or she pushes.

 Skills necessary: You need to be comfortable discussing sensitive financial topics with your clients, and in turn, your clients need to feel comfortable with you. Being a "people" person will go a long way in this field. You'll also need to become certified by a financial planning trade association to gain credibility with clients.

 Investment required: Low.

 For more information: Financial Planning Association, 4100 East Mississippi Avenue, Suite 400, Denver, CO 80246-3053; 800-322-4237; *www.fpanet.org*

Some people love to go over their personal investments with a fine-toothed comb and jump on hot stock tips whenever a news item comes across the wire. Others would love to do this, but don't have the time. Still others choose to keep an ear to the ground for breaking financial news, but would rather delegate the task of assembling a financial portfolio to someone else.

All three of these categories of people are prime candidates to work with a financial planner, whose job it is to keep abreast not only of the day-to-day financial markets, but to also make educated investment decisions based on the different needs of their clients, whether it's saving for retirement, buying a house, or putting kids through college—all three of which, increasingly, need to be considered simultaneously when making financial decisions.

Many financial planners charge an hourly fee, but most make their money off the commissions they earn from serving as a stockbroker and selling insurance and other financial products to clients. Taking the time to explain complex financial issues to clients may not seem like the best way to build your own financial-planning business, but the loyalty you'll win from people who appreciate that you can listen to their concerns is the best way to do it in the long run.

76. Personal Fitness Training

 Description of the business: A business where a fitness trainer works one-on-one with clients, either at a public gym or at a client's home.

Why it's a good business to start if you don't want to work hard anymore: People will continue to be interested in staying healthy with regular exercise, but they are increasingly looking to private sessions to maintain fitness and motivation as more events compete for their attention and energy. It's easy to develop a clientele where you can work for a few hours in the morning, and then another late-afternoon session, leaving you not only fit but with a lot of spare time.

 Skills necessary: A B.A. in physical fitness helps, though several years of fitness instruction in another field will suffice; you'll need to be a great motivator and entertainer to keep clients up and coming back.

 Investment required: Low.

 For more information: IDEA Health & Fitness Association, 10455 Pacific Center Court, San Diego, CA 92121; 858-535-8979; *www.ideafit.com*

Despite some lapses, Americans are as gung ho about keeping fit and staying in shape as ever. The only problem is that despite this enthusiasm, there frequently seems to be something that comes up to sideswipe your best intentions to make it into the gym that day.

Enter the personal fitness trainer, whose job it is to cajole clients into doing just one more situp and when to lay it on thick as well as when it's time to slack off. If you've always loved to exercise and would love nothing more than to spend your entire day sweating and helping other people succeed, then becoming a personal fitness trainer is a great choice. It's not easy, and even if you've spent your entire life in great shape, the constant motion involved in training eight to 10 clients in the course of one day can cause you to crawl into bed every night.

But there's nothing more rewarding, whether you work out a deal to train clients at a local gym or drive to their houses to put them through the paces in their own home gyms. If you have a great personality and can keep clients smiling all the way through a grueling 45-minute workout, then it's likely that other fitness buffs will find their way to you. After all, that's how the stars of fitness videos got started: by teaching classes and giving private training sessions.

77. Personal Shopping Service

Description of the business: A business that shops for gifts and other items for consumers and businesspeople.

Why it's a good business to start if you don't want to work hard anymore: Many people lack the time to brave the crowds and traffic to shop for a present or necessity; others don't know where to look for a particular item, so a professional shopper who can do all this and more is a valuable service.

Skills necessary: You must love to shop and not accept negative answers in the search for a must-have item.

Investment required: Low.

For more information: *FabJob Guide to Become a Personal Shopper,* e-book by Laura Harrison McBride and Peter J. Gallanis; *www.fabjob.com*

On the surface, it sounds a bit ludicrous: getting paid to go shopping. Yet, there are millions of people who would be happy to let you do just that, as long as you are able to find the item in question in the time frame provided. Despite the proliferation of online shopping venues, searching for just the right item on the Internet encompasses many of the same frustrations inherent in traditional shopping: You have to know where to look, and then you have to wait for it to arrive. Enter the personal shopper, you, with a Rolodex crammed with little-known boutiques and shops where you can purchase even the most obscure item and have it delivered the next day, while your client thinks you sweated hours to find just the right thing.

Whether it's gifts, food, or clothes, personal shoppers possess a savvy and the instincts of a bloodhound when it comes to locating a discontinued piece of china or a fruitcake with dried—not candied—cherries, made by a company that your client couldn't remember. Although some clients employ a personal shopper only once in awhile, a number of executive women will hire a personal shopper to purchase a new wardrobe or a few new items of clothing with the coming of each new season, once the shopper is familiar with a client's taste, size, and lifestyle.

If your license plate says "Born to Shop," starting a personal shopping business will make it seem like you're in heaven.

78. Pet Specialty Manufacturing

 Description of the business: A business that produces toys, accessories, and/or foods for pets.

 Why it's a good business to start if you don't want to work hard anymore: The pet industry has grown by leaps and bounds in recent years as people lavish more attention on their household pets, buying them upscale toys and beds, having them groomed regularly, even taking them to camps and spas.

 Skills necessary: You have to love pets and you should possess an eye for what pet lovers will buy for their best friends.

 Investment required: Low.

 For more information: *Pet Age* magazine, 200 S. Michigan Avenue, Chicago, IL 60604; 312-663-4040; *www.petage.com*

Today, more than ever, people are spoiling their pets—dogs, cats, ferrets, and iguanas—which has created a huge growth opportunity for pet-loving entrepreneurs who want to focus their business around their passion. Whether it's greeting cards, hand-made catnip toys, or waterproof clothes for dogs, the specialty pet business is booming, and the great thing about the industry is that it's lot of fun, and you can bring your pets with you on business calls. After all, what better testimony than straight from the horse's mouth?

Before you focus on a particular type of toy or other item to produce, you should take a look at the products that are already on the market and flying off the shelf. Next, ask yourself how you can make your own idea fit into the existing market while standing out on the crowded shelves. After all, the world doesn't need another company that makes dog leashes. One company makes catnip toys patterned after people that cats love to hate, such as the vet or the mean kid next door. Although your product will ultimately have to appeal to the pet, you first have to catch the eye of the human who is owned by that pet.

If you're an animal lover, you're already more than halfway towards having what it takes to run a successful specialty pet business. Your own in-house animal staff will be more than happy to serve on the board of directors; the good news is that they usually work cheap.

79. Pet-sitting Service

 Description of the business: An entrepreneur who visits a client's home to take care of the pets while the client is traveling.

 Why it's a good business to start if you don't want to work hard anymore: People are taking more, briefer trips and vacations. They're also treating their pets more like children, and would prefer they remain in familiar surroundings if the owner has to go away for a period of time. You'll need to visit the pets at least twice a day, leaving the rest of your time free.

 Skills necessary: It helps if you get along better with dogs and cats than with people.

 Investment required: Low.

For more information: *Pet Sitting for Profit: A Complete Manual for Professional Success,* by Patti J. Moran (John Wiley, 1997).

If you're always the person that cats and dogs come to sniff the first time you visit a new friend's house and if you would rather spend time talking with the animals than with their owners, pet-sitting would be a great choice for you.

Pet-sitting is an easy business to start and run. The majority of clients will be dogs and cats, but there is also the occasional pot-bellied pig or iguana to tend. Pet sitters need to keep their early mornings and late afternoons/early evenings free to visit a home to put out fresh food and water, walk the dog, clean the litter box, and throw a few toys—all of which can usually be accomplished in less than a half hour per visit.

Some clients will want you to stay at the house overnight, in which case you'd be house-sitting, along with pet-sitting. If your own living situation allows for this, you'd essentially be getting paid to sleep, which is great work if you can get it.

As is the case with other pet-care businesses, pet-sitting can be combined with another pet-related service, allowing you to increase your potential customer base as well as the amount of business you can get from each of your existing customers. Before you start your pet-sitting business, however, take a look at the sitters who are already offering their services in your area. Because this is such an easy and inexpen-sive business to start, there may be stiff competition from the beginning. But if you take care to set your business apart in some way—such as guaranteeing you'll pay a minimum of 20 minutes of attention to the pet on each visit—and then collect an impressive roster of references, your business will stand out among the others.

80. Pooper Scooper Business

 Description of the business: An entrepreneur visits a dog owner's home every week or so to remove dog waste from the yard.

 Why it's a good business to start if you don't want to work hard anymore: People are working longer hours and commuting longer distances. They are required to keep their dogs outside in an enclosed area for lengthy periods of time, and the last thing they want to do in their spare time is to pick up dog litter. They'll pay a premium for the service.

 Skills necessary: A sense of humor and a strong stomach.

 Investment required: Low.

? **For more information:** International Directory of Dog Waste Removal Services, 2893 Brownlee Avenue, Columbus, OH 43209; *www.pooper-scooper.com*

Scoop & Poop, Doggie Doo, Mary Poopins—the best part of starting a pooper scooper business *has* to be coming up with an inventive name that will catch people's attention. Seriously, though, a pooper scooper business is a great business to run part-time and in a suburban area where the majority of families are not at home during the day. It's not rocket science, however, and aside from purchasing a good supply of garbage bags, a shovel, a rake, and several pair of gloves, a pooper scooper business is probably the cheapest business you could start.

Finding clients is easy. You can post fliers at the supermarket, local animal shelters, and even let veterinarians and pet shops know of your service. Of course, it helps if you love dogs, but the fact that

a pooper scooper business is frequently a part-time venture means that it's very easy to combine this service with another pet-related business and market both of them at the same time. For instance, on the day you visit a particular client, you can also offer your dog-walking services, or turn into a pet sitter when the same client needs to go out of town, thus increasing your revenue stream.

Of course it's a business that people will poke fun at, but once the laughter stops, many of them will ask if you can visit their homes to take care of their dog yards as well.

81. Professional Organizing

 Description of the business: A service in which you help an individual or a business make order out of chaos at their home or office.

 Why it's a good business to start if you don't want to work hard anymore: The concept of hiring a professional to help organize home and work space is beginning to catch on, plus Americans will only become busier and have less time in coming years.

 Skills necessary: A sense of order and logic are good skills to possess. The ability to organize items into easily accessible categories is a must.

 Investment required: Low.

 For more information: National Association of Professional Organizers, 4700 West Lake Avenue, Glenview, IL 60025; 847-375-4746; *www.napo.net*

People know they should have a well-organized desk or closet. The problem is that they often lack the time and ability to do it themselves. That's where a professional organizer comes in—not only to arrange files and shoes in homes and offices, but to continue helping to keep clients well organized by tweaking their systems and by being firm yet sympathetic when someone reverts to old methods of behavior.

Most professional organizers report that their primary market consists of executive men and women who lack the time and foresight to get their papers and files into a logical order, both in the office and at home. However, one surprising aspect of the job of a professional organizer is that it often involves creating order not only in the office, but also in a person's busy schedule, putting effective time-management skills and advice to work. Many people are incapable of managing their flow of paperwork, and they're often equally inefficient when it comes to managing time. As a result, professional organizers are often called upon to perform a complete overhaul. A patient constitution combined with a good deal of hand-holding and psychological aptitude are welcome traits of professional organizers.

You may choose to work primarily with individuals or corporate clients. If you do a good job in one area, you may well be called on to perform your magic at a client's other domain. In fact, your goal is to be so good that your talents are no longer needed—at least with that client. It's a messy world out there; professional organizers already have their hands full.

82. Public Relations Consulting

 Description of the business: A venture that promotes businesses and individuals by getting them mentioned in newspapers and magazines, on radio and television programs, and online.

 Why it's a good business to start if you don't want to work hard anymore: Advertising is getting more expensive, and media people are getting overwhelmed with submissions. It helps to hire a professional publicist to break through the noise. If you can place clients in national media, your higher fees will be justified.

 Skills necessary: If you're creative, good on the phone, and can come up with an endless variety of ways to position your clients, you should do well in public relations.

 Investment required: Low.

 For more information: The Public Relations Society of America, 33 Irving Place, New York, NY 10003; 212-995-2230; *www.prsa.org*

The ironic thing about opening up a business as a public relations consultant is that, if you're good at it, word will spread quickly, and it won't be necessary for you to develop a publicity campaign to promote your own business—you'll be too busy working for your clients.

Public relations consultants get a lot of flack for trying to place fluffy stories with no news quotient, but the truth is that the battalion of national-, regional-, and local-media people relies on publicity experts to point them in the direction of new trends and potentially newsworthy stories. As the amount of information that crosses a reporter's desk in the

course of one day could easily take one month to plow through, a harried, overworked reporter on deadline will be especially receptive to an angle from a publicist who will help his audience and make him look good to his bosses at the same time.

A public relations consultant gets clients into the media by making initial contact with a reporter by sending a press release and then following up with a phone call. Having a lot of contacts and a good track record of newsworthy ideas helps because an editor or producer is more likely to take a publicist's advice. After all, the best public relations consultants do their homework about whether or not the client would fit into a specific format or angle. Consultants are frequently offering up preselected sources for a reporter to interview, along with several story angles as well.

It's getting increasingly important for a business to get mentioned in the media. Skilled public relations consultants will only thrive in this environment.

83. Recycling Pick-up

 Description of the business: A business that picks up recyclable materials from homes and offices to bring to recycling centers on a regular basis.

 Why it's a good business to start if you don't want to work hard anymore: Most cities and towns instituted rigid recycling policies in the 1990s. In many places, the municipality doesn't pick up recyclables, leaving the task to the homeowner or business owner, who usually lacks the time and desire.

 Skills necessary: You'll need to be well-organized and prompt, because most people are accustomed to having their trash picked up at the same time on the same day every week.

 Investment required: Medium.

 For more information: *Scrap* magazine, 1325 G Street NW, Washington, DC 20005; 202-737-1770; *www.scrap.org*

"Save the planet" was the battle cry of the 1990s. However, when the time came to put words into actions, many people and business owners balked at the thought of squeezing yet another task into an already over-crowded schedule. As is the case with many of the everyday chores that busy people can now hire someone else to perform, picking up recyclables, such as bottles, cans, and newspapers (usually on a weekly basis), is now another service business that people will gladly pay for.

Many commercial recycling pick-up services, however, work with recycling centers that accomodate commercial operations, not individual residents who drop off only a few plastic milk jugs and a week's worth of newspapers. A recycling pick-up business requires no special skills, just a truck large enough to carry everything, and an agreement with the proprietor of a local recycling center—although it may be the town dump or landfill—to dispose of the recyclables there. You may need to secure a special permit from the town and may need to schedule a special drop-off time so as not to interfere with other residents.

84. Relocation Consulting

 Description of the business: A consultant assists individuals and businesses in planning a physical move, which could include packing boxes, contracting a moving company, even renting a home in the new location.

 Why it's a good business to start if you don't want to work hard anymore: We are a mobile society; 20 percent of people change addresses every year, and many are too busy to handle the details and logistics of moving themselves. If you live in an area of high mobility, people will pay a premium to ease the moving process.

 Skills necessary: You'll need to be good at handling details and organizing the move, from A to Z, as well as smoothing feathers when something goes wrong.

 Investment required: Medium.

 For more information: Employee Relocation Council, 1717 Pennsylvania Avenue NW, Suite 800, Washington, DC 20006; 202-857-0857; *www.erc.org*

Relocation consultants are take-charge people who can turn on a dime and employ bully tactics or diplomatic negotiations, depending upon the situation. Although corporations often hire relocation consultants to smooth the process of moving an employee to another location, individuals are using their services in increasing numbers because they don't have the time or energy it takes to move an entire household, whether it's across the country or across town.

Relocation consultants need to be well connected, especially within the local moving industry, and good at pulling strings whenever possible. Perfectionists need not apply. Have you ever moved your household and had everything go off without a hitch? Relocation consultants don't necessarily have better track records, they're just better at smoothing over the mistakes and recognizing the signs before they can snowball, whether it's a broken down truck or an inventory list that comes up short.

If you decide to take this route, don't be surprised if your clients tend to reveal the most intimate details of their lives to you. After all, a relocation consultant is taking full responsibility for moving what is frequently a person's entire collection of worldly goods—you'd be nervous too.

85. Restaurateur

 Description of the business: A business that serves meals to people. It may specialize in a particular kind of cuisine, such as Italian, or one kind of food, such as a café with light snacks.

 Why it's a good business to start if you don't want to work hard anymore: All studies indicate that the trend towards eating more meals out will continue growing over the coming years. More people consider cooking to be appropriate for a special occasion and will instead rely on take-out and restaurant meals on a regular basis.

 Skills necessary: Cooking skills help, but a strong business sense is more important, including filling a local demand with food and service that keeps customers coming back.

 Investment required: High.

 **For more information:** National Restaurant Association, 1200 17th Street NW, Washington, DC 20036; 202-331-5900; *www.restaurant.org*

Ask anyone who loves to cook for a hobby, and chances are that they dream of running their own restaurant. While this passion will go a long way towards ensuring a restaurant's eventual success, the truth is that you can be the greatest cook in the world, but if you neglect the business side of running a restaurant—an industry with notoriously thin profit margins—you won't last long.

That's why restaurants are frequently run as partnerships, with one person responsible for the kitchen while the other keeps the books and does the behind-the-scenes work. After all, many chefs are artists, a group of people who tend to not want to deal with the business issues of their craft.

The good news is that the restaurant business is booming and should continue to do so, despite the economy. Many people with little spare time would rather spend their free hours relaxing or participating in outside pursuits, not preparing dinner for the brood. And because people have to eat at least something each day, there will always be a market for good food served with a smile, in the kind of atmosphere that allows people to let down their hair and tune the world out for a while. If you envision the same kind of restaurant and aren't afraid of more hard work than you'll know—although many restaurateurs don't view it as work—you should follow your dream.

86. Reunion Planning

 Description of the business: A service that organizes and produces reunions for families, classes, and other social groups that want to gather together.

 Why it's a good business to start if you don't want to work hard anymore: The Internet is making it easier to stay in touch, but ironically, it increases the desire for more face-to-face contact. Few people have the time to plan and pull off a full-fledged reunion, which leaves the market open for professional planners.

 Skills necessary: You should be well organized, know how to throw a great party, and have the nose of a bloodhound to track down far-flung contacts.

 Investment required: Low.

? **For more information:**
National Association of Reunion Managers, PO Box 23211, Tampa, FL 33623; 800-654-2776; *www.reunions.com*
or:
Reunions Magazine, PO Box 11727, Milwaukee, WI 53211; 414-263-4567; *www.reunionsmag.com*

Though the idea of a class or family reunion strikes fear in the hearts of more than a few people, the truth is that it's a booming business, with 150,000 gatherings held for classmates, families, and military units each year. The majority of reunions are thrown together by members of that particular group, though I'd guess a vast majority would not hesitate to hand the reins over to a professional to take care of the details and time-consuming tasks.

Enter the professional reunion planner, who attends to the details from A to Z, locating long-lost group members; booking the venue, caterer, and band; and designing and sending out the invitations. The planner will also attend the function to make sure that everything runs smoothly; this total control means that those who are attending the reunion as guests can relax and enjoy themselves.

This business is not for the weak of heart, however, because a reunion planner must be able to deal with a variety of personalities and take charge during unpleasant occasions, all in the quest to pull off a successful reunion. If you can keep the big picture in sight at all times, while staying on top of the little things that will make people remember the event for years to come, becoming a reunion planner is a good choice.

87. Sales Rep Service

 Description of the business: An enterprise that sells products and/or services for other companies, earning a commission on all sales.

 Why it's a good business to start if you don't want to work hard anymore: Good salespeople are hard to find. If you like to sell and prefer to juggle a variety of products and/or services for different companies—and you're good at it— there are many companies that would like to bring you on board.

 Skills necessary: Obviously, you need to be able to sell effectively and enjoy spending time with people. Good organizational skills also help.

 Investment required: Low.

 For more information: *Sales: Building Lifetime Skills for Success,* by Bob Mander (Ryan & Company, 1999).

Most people crinkle up their noses when they're asked to sell everything from raffle tickets to Girl Scout cookies. However, if you love to sell, you probably already know that your skills are highly prized. But if you like being able to sell products and services for a number of different companies as an independent sales rep, you don't have to represent just one manufacturer to hold what frequently amounts to nothing more than a staff position.

It's possible for you to build a thriving sales firm by representing several different non-competing companies and make more money on the road—or by selling from home via direct mail and a Website—than you could by limiting the number of items you sell. Once you build a reputation, along with your territory, you can bring on more sales reps to generate even more revenue for both you and the companies you represent.

Many sales reps decide to go off on their own for the same reasons that non-sales-oriented employees do: They want to be able to sell a product or service in their own personal style. Many companies want their staff salespeople either to push certain products or hold back from utilizing certain methods. But being a successful salesperson means the ability to forge prosperous, lasting relationships. Starting your own independent sales rep business means you'll be able to forge your relationships in your own way and on your own terms, full speed ahead.

88. Secretarial Service

 Description of the business: A business that provides a variety of secretarial services—from word-processing and transcription to envelope stuffing and faxing—to businesses, on a contract basis.

 Why it's a good business to start if you don't want to work hard anymore: The number of one-person businesses will grow, and while these enterprises need occasional secretarial help, there isn't enough work to keep an assistant on staff. Freelance secretaries can work remotely.

 Skills necessary: Fast and accurate typing and an understanding of general office procedures are necessary, as well as the inclination to pitch in on other projects.

 Investment required: Low.

? **For more information:** *Up Close & Virtual: A Practical Guide to Starting Your Own Virtual Assistant Business,* by Diana Ennen and Kelly Poelker (Ennen's Computer Services, 2003).

With the personal computer being a necessary piece of equipment in most offices these days, it's no longer necessary to hire a person to "take a letter" because it's likely the executive in need of the service would do it himself.

As more offices convert their secretaries into the position of administrative assistants (more accurately describe their responsibilities), it sometimes seems that secretaries will soon be extinct. Of course, nothing could be further from the truth. Their skills are still in demand, it's just that an average executive or businessowner may need fewer of a secretary's talents less often. A secretarial service is available when needed, without the bother and expense of training a temporary employee or the need to furnish a desk.

It's possible that a secretarial service can do work for companies all over the world that transmit their handwritten notes or letters in need of editing by fax or e-mail. The service then prints it out on the company's letterhead—again, transmitted electronically if necessary—and sends it out with the letter writer's electronic signature.

Of course a secretarial entrepreneur may still have to employ the old-fashioned kinds of skills—such as dictation—but increasingly, computers and electronic communication give them a newfangled twist.

89. Seminar Leader

 Description of the business: Conducting seminars, workshops, and lectures on a specific subject to a paying audience, either locally or nationally.

 Why it's a good business to start if you don't want to work hard anymore: People are flocking to workshops and seminars where a charismatic and knowledgeable teacher can provide them with the information they need to improve their personal and work lives and will often pay handsomely for the service.

 Skills necessary: You must be an entertainer, as well as a teacher, in order to succeed. It's also vital for you to be a "people" person, have boundless energy, and to know your subject inside and out.

 Investment required: Medium.

 For more information: American Seminar Leaders Association, 2405 E. Washington Boulevard, Pasadena, CA 91104; 800-735-0511; *www.asla.com*

Do you like teaching people? Do you enjoy being an entertainer for an afternoon, day, week, or longer, keeping your energy up along with the spirits of the people you're teaching? Starting a seminar business can be a great way to educate people on a subject you know well, whether it's gardening, finding a job or a mate, even training llamas. Whether you produce, market, and host a seminar, or just agree to show up on the appointed day and leave all the details to a producer or related business in your field, if you have a penchant for being the center of attention and can make people laugh and learn simultaneously, starting a business as a seminar leader can be a lucrative way to be in the spotlight and get your ideas out there at the same time.

Of course, it helps if you've already built a name for yourself as an expert in your particular field, but if you have information and advice to pass along and people are willing to pay a fee to get you to teach them, you should be able to succeed as a seminar leader.

Seminar leaders—both famous and little-known—can make big bucks. The best leaders consider themselves to be as much performers as trainers. Because marketing to a previous, satisfied customer is cheaper and easier than going after a prospective client who may not be familiar with the value of taking a seminar with you—unless you're Deepak Chopra, of course—many seminar leaders quickly learn that they have to constantly develop new seminars to keep people coming back. But seeing the changes that are possible in people, solely due to your efforts, is the best reward of being a seminar leader.

90. Software Development

 Description of the business: An entrepreneur develops, designs, and programs software, to meet the needs of a particular company or industry, and may also work to adapt existing software to better serve the business and employees.

 Why it's a good business to start if you don't want to work hard anymore: Companies of all sizes and in all fields are hungry for skilled developers and programmers to customize their software, to streamline their office operations.

 Skills necessary: A background and a degree in programming are necessary. The ability to project how a particular program is used in a business setting can help you to make suggestions that nontechnical employees would have trouble seeing.

 Investment required: Medium.

 For more information: Software Development Forum, III West Saint John, Suite 200, San Jose, CA 95113; 408-494-8378; *www.center.org*

Software developers are in high demand across the board. The situation has gotten to the point that companies don't care if they hire full-time staff or outside consultants, just as long as the job gets done, which is good news for developers and programmers who want to strike out on their own.

Although a developer may initially design the parameters for the software (leaving the actual programming to another software consultant), many developers are expected to do it all, from overseeing outside coding work to checking the prototype for bugs and glitches, to communicating with the employees who will actually be using the software on a daily basis.

In fact, things have gotten so desperate in some industries and corporations that they are hiring and training people who have but an elementary knowledge of software development and programming, just so the work gets done, albeit more slowly. If you want to get into software development (even if you lack any formal training in programming), first spending a couple of years getting paid a salary by a corporation, while you learn the ropes, may be just the thing that enables you to go out on your own sometime down the road.

91. Systems Analysis

 Description of the business: An individual examines the computer systems and networks in a company and makes recommendations for new hardware and software to help meet the company's needs.

 Why it's a good business to start if you don't want to work hard anymore: Many computer professionals specialize in one area. Systems analysts are generalists, trained to keep the big picture in mind while suggesting alterations to the components. Most computer education tells students to focus on the *trees*, not the *forest*, although both are equally important.

 Skills necessary: Being computer savvy and having a detective's mind and curiosity are necessary, as well as knowing how different software and hardware interact with each other.

 Investment required: Low.

 For more information: Society for Information Management, 401 N. Michigan Avenue, Chicago, IL 60611; 312-527-6734; *www.simnet.org*

For years, the term *systems analyst* has been tossed around corporate America. No one knew exactly what they did, but people did realize that they helped determine how effective a company's computer systems were, which went toward increasing efficiency and ultimately, the bottom line.

Systems analysts are responsible for determining how well a company's network of computers meets its original goals. This may involve not only pure analysis that matches the goals up with actual performance, but also with adding new software and tweaking existing programs, as well as figuring out the best way to make separate computers able to communicate with each other. They may design a computer system from start to finish, interview both the people who will work on the system and the executives who steer the course of the company, and occasionally be required to write new programs that will best help the company to meet its goals—all the while keeping up with constantly changing technology.

If you're a computer professional and don't want to focus on one aspect of information technology, starting a business as a systems analyst will allow you to serve as the conductor of the computer systems for one or more companies.

92. Tax Consulting

Description of the business: Preparing tax returns for individuals, small businesses, and corporations.

Why it's a good business to start if you don't want to work hard anymore: U.S. tax code is going to continue to become more complicated, and more people who have traditionally prepared their own returns are going to turn to outside help, out of frustration. You can make this a highly seasonal business, working the first third of the year and taking the rest of the time off.

Skills necessary: It's a good idea to take tax-preparation classes and become certified as a tax preparer by your state. Annual courses to update you on new changes in tax law are always a good option.

Investment required: Low.

For more information: *Getting Started in Tax Consulting,* by Gary W. Carter, (John Wiley, 2001).

Are you among the few Americans who always got a secret thrill doing your own taxes? And were you good enough at it that your family and friends noticed and asked you to do theirs as well? Well, you might as well get paid for it. And the best way to get a foot in the door of your own tax preparation business is by taking advantage of an apprenticeship offered by your local H&R Block tax preparation office. You can either sign up for their tax preparation classes and work at their offices for one season, learning the intricacies and variety of tax situations that exist out there— that is, if you're good enough that they offer you a job—or else just take the classes and hang out your own shingle.

Of course, computerized tax preparation software has made it easier to completely fill out a tax return, whether it's your own or those of hundreds of your own clients, making it absolutely essential to purchase an updated copy of Intuit TurboTax or another tax-preparation program every year, because they automatically apply any changes in tax laws to the formula.

They also cut down on the amount of flipping back through old records that you'll have to do, because they provide automatic figures, such as on those items a client is depreciating over the course of several years, for instance.

93. Technical Support

Description of the business: A business that provides support and troubleshooting for computer users over the phone, via e-mail, or in person.

Why it's a good business to start if you don't want to work hard anymore: People are impatient when it comes to figuring out a software glitch themselves or calling the manufacturer's help line. If they can call somebody they know will help, many people and businesses would gladly pay for the service.

Skills necessary: A knowledge of a variety of commonly used software, the ability to communicate clearly and simply with clients, and patience with stupid questions.

Investment required: Low.

For more information: Association of Computer Support Specialists, 333 Mamaroneck Avenue #129, White Plains, NY 10605; 914-713-7222; *www.acss.org*

If you can keep your cool and clearly explain things when a frazzled computer user reports that he thought the CD drive was a cup holder, you have a bright future running a technical support service. The first thing to decide, however, is whether you want to be a generalist, covering a number of different software programs, or focus on one industry, using a specific kind and brand of software.

When it comes to technical support, people on both sides have their horror stories, from the customer telling of the time he was put on hold for an hour to the support specialist rolling her eyes at the ignorance of some callers. If you can provide efficient and friendly advice while treating a confused caller with respect, you'll quickly build up a bustling business. Some support specialists focus on corporations and charge a monthly retainer, in exchange for agreeing to accept a specific number of calls during that time. Others choose to charge by the minute. Many tech support entrepreneurs "cut their teeth" by manning the help hotlines of major software manufacturers, which is a great way to train.

Some support businesses focus on a particular brand of software that's particularly tricky—such as some of the graphic design programs with more bells and whistles than most users are even aware of—while some like to be generalists. In either case, realize that the need for computer technical support, in all its guises, is never going to go away. And that's good news for support entrepreneurs everywhere.

94. Technical Writing

 Description of the business: A service in which a writer creates documents and manuals to clearly convey technical information and instructions to the reader.

 Why it's a good business to start if you don't want to work hard anymore: With thousands of new software programs appearing on the market every year, not to mention appliances, vehicles, or anything else that requires a clear set of instructions to operate, technical writers will always be in demand.

 Skills necessary: You'll need the ability to translate technical jargon into sentences that are easy for the target end user to understand, and you must be good at meeting deadlines.

 Investment required: Low.

For more information: The Society for Technical Communication, 901 North Stuart Street, Suite 904, Arlington, VA 22203; 703-522-4114; *www.stc.org*

If you can write clearly and concisely and are able to explain complex technical issues to the common layperson, using nontechnical terms, then you'll always have work as a technical writer. Though some projects require specialized knowledge in a particular field, many technical writers are able to apply their skills to most industries, from computer hardware and software documentation to large appliance owner's manuals. Obviously, if you have a well-developed technical acumen, you'll be able to write more quickly and accurately.

The good thing about running a technical writing business is that you can do it from anywhere. The internet, e-mail, and overnight delivery services mean that you can live 3,000 miles or more from your clients. And the demand for technical writers is only expected to build as people and industries all over the world become more comfortable with a continued increase in technology in daily life. After all, someone has to make it make sense to them.

95. Translating Service

 Description of the business: A business that translates documents and spoken word from one language into another.

 Why it's a good business to start if you don't want to work hard anymore: As more countries and businesses start to trade and exchange information on a global basis, they will need individuals to translate their conversation for them. Your skills can command a high price, even if you perform the work on a remote basis.

 Skills necessary: You'll need to be fluent in writing and/or speaking at least one foreign language.

 Investment required: Low.

 For more information: American Translators Association, 225 Reinekers Lane, Alexandria, VA 22314; 703-683-6100; *www.atanet.org*

As the world becomes more populated and developed, the lines of communication between cultures shorten, which presents a bevy of opportunities for those who are able to help people who speak different languages communicate with each other.

Many people are surprised to discover that many skilled translators perform only spoken or written translations, not both. Many translators also prefer to communicate in one direction. This is good news for those who are fluent in a language, but who are more comfortable when they write than when they speak, for instance, or who are more comfortable translating from Spanish to English than translating English to Spanish.

Despite a translator's own personal preferences, there is a growing abundance of work for everyone. A translator may be called upon to work in tandem with a tour guide, to translate legal documents, or to even consult with traveling executives about the cultural differences between two countries.

Translators may work directly with governments, the news media, law firms, and marketing agencies, among other industries. Regardless of the chosen niche, the market for independent translators should only grow as the distance between worlds shrinks.

96. Used Book Dealing

Description of the business: A business that sells used books, occasionally offering other merchandise.

Why it's a good business to start if you don't want to work hard anymore: Despite the proliferation of online bookstores selling new and used books, people still want to visit brick-and-mortar stores where they can leisurely wander the aisles and leaf through books before they buy them.

Skills necessary: If you love books, a used bookstore is a good option.

Investment required: Low.

For more information: *Book Finds: How to Find, Buy, and Sell Used and Rare Books,* by Ian C. Ellis (Perigee, 2001).

Book lovers are a breed apart from other folks, but used-book lovers are a species unto themselves. Many used bookstore owners get into the business because they have too many books, and want an excuse to keep buying more. The majority start out in the business buying books they like, though the smart ones, who don't want to starve, quickly learn that a lot of the books they like don't sell at all.

Frequently, used bookstore owners are asked by customers to do a search for some relatively obscure books; more than one used bookstore owner compares the process to throwing a message in a bottle into the ocean—one in four searches is considered to be a success.

However, with the advent of technology, used bookstore owners are casting a wide net for their searches and coming up with great finds more often than in the pre-Internet olden days. In fact, many used bookstore owners are now deriving an increasing percentage of their revenues from Internet sales. Not only are they selling to customers all over the world via their own Website, but they're serving as inventory for the huge online bookstores, such as Amazon, which also sell used books. When they receive a request from a customer on a particular used book, Amazon will send out an e-mail to their network of used bookstores for the book's availability, as well as the lowest price.

Used bookstores may seem to have the future of a dinosaur, given all the whirlwind technology swirling around them, but in reality, technology may be just the thing to *save* them and make this a thriving business for lovers of old books.

97. Website Design

Description of the business: Planning and designing the look of a Website for a company or individual.

Why it's a good business to start if you don't want to work hard anymore: The Internet isn't going anywhere, and its influence over American commerce and communication will continue to grow. Talented designers who can help a Website stand out will be in high demand.

Skills necessary: A graphic arts background helps, as well as familiarity with Web design programs and coding.

Investment required: Medium.

For more information: Web Design and Developers Association, 8515 Brower, Houston, TX 77017; 435-518-9784; *www.wdda.org*

We live in a world where the eye dictates and the brain and the body follow. This is especially true on the Internet, where visitors to a Web page can determine in less than a second if a particular site is worth investigating in depth. A picture is worth a lot more than a thousand words, in this case.

Designing for the Web involves a whole new way of thinking for designers. Taking advantage of the typically short attention span of many Internet users requires the use of certain graphics, colors, and fonts, as well as attention to the overall presentation. Graphic artists view the Web as a free-for-all, a medium in which they are least constricted when it comes to their brainstorms and ideas.

A Web designer will become a more integral part of the entire process as time passes. Each of the tasks involved in getting a Website up and running used to be handled by a generalist. Today, a team of very talented specialists working together but in their own little niche is more the rule, and in turn, each skill category will continue to branch off into even more directions.

The rate of change in the online world is so quick and dramatic that no one can predict how the Internet will be shaping lives 10 months from now, let alone 10 years. But this is a good thing. Even if other job categories come and go, the designer will be one of only a handful of mainstays. After all, you can tell a Website by its home page.

98. Website Development

 Description of the business: An entrepreneur conceives and plans a Website appropriate for a client, acting as conductor and mastermind of the whole project.

 Why it's a good business to start if you don't want to work hard anymore: With all of the tasks divided up between people and businesses with very specific skills, someone still needs to serve as a ring leader, who sees both the trees and the forest.

 Skills necessary: You'll need to know how a Website will best serve a client's needs and be familiar with all the parts of a Website, from the shopping cart program to the use of applets, as well as its overall flow.

 Investment required: Medium.

 For more information: Web Design and Developers Association, 8515 Brower, Houston, TX 77017; 435-518-9784; *www.wdda.org*

A Website developer serves as the line between two radically different factions: the corporation, which wants its Website to do the company justice, and the Web design and coding side, which can be pretty territorial about the best way to create a Website from scratch.

A Web developer, therefore, must be able to fluently speak two different languages—corporate speak and hip Internet speak—and effortlessly translate between the two without stumbling. Although a developer can feasibly work alone on the project, she most often serves as a general contractor of sorts, assembling the teams of specialists who will work together to create a seamless product.

The developer interviews the company in depth to discover what it is they want their Website to accomplish, who they want it to reach, and the revenue they want it to generate. She must then take this information and convey it to a team of writers, designers, and programmers. Once work commences, the developer continues to serve as a go-between for these two diametrically opposed sides. Once the Website is completed to everyone's satisfaction, it's time to let the world know it's there. Again, this may involve an outside contractor, an in-house online marketing specialist, or even the Website developer.

Developers love to juggle, and also have a passion for the ever-changing landscape of the World Wide Web. After all, it keeps them on their toes.

99. Wedding Planning

 Description of the business: A business that handles the planning and logistics for a wedding and all the details leading up to it.

 Why it's a good business to start if you don't want to work hard anymore: Many of the people inclined to have big weddings seem to have the least amount of time to plan them and are likely to hire a service to do it.

 Skills necessary: You'll need good organization and research skills, an eye for style, and a flair for negotiation and diplomacy.

 Investment required: Low.

 For more information: Association of Certified Professional Wedding Consultants, 7791 Prestwick Circle, San Jose, CA 95135; 408-528-9000; *www.acpwc.com*

Humans are the eternal optimists and seem to believe that the fancier the wedding, the greater the odds that the marriage will make it. The wedding planner is the great conductor whose job it is to make sure that everyone goes away happy and that these grand events are flawless.

A wedding planner works with a couple and asks a million questions about their taste in cake, flowers, music, food, wedding vows, venues—you get the idea. They also work with suppliers—from florist to printer that create the invitations—to extract from them the best service and/or product at the best price. As well, they will work with the caterer or band to make sure they are aware of all of the little personalized details that will be the icing on the cake of the couple's wedding day, so to speak. As a result, if anything goes wrong, the planner must be prepared to take the heat and do whatever it takes to make it right. A wedding planner can be paid either a percentage of the total estimated wedding cost or on an hourly basis.

It's a tough job, but somebody has to do it. If you're the type of person who always loved planning the party more than the party itself and you're a romantic at heart, who loves happy endings, then becoming a wedding planner would be a good choice.

100. Window Washing

 Description of the business: A business that cleans windows, inside and out, for residential and commercial customers.

 Why it's a good business to start if you don't want to work hard anymore: An increase in residential and commercial construction in many parts of the country means more opportunities for window washers. This can be a high-paying seasonal job in many parts of the country.

 Skills necessary: An eye for detail, perfectionism, and strength—in order to handle the scaffolding—not to mention the lack of a fear of heights.

 Investment required: Low.

 For more information: International Window Cleaning Association, 6418 Grovedale Drive, #101B, Alexandria, VA 22310; 800-875-4922; *www.iwca.org*

If you like to work outside, physically exert yourself, and enjoy having a view of the world that few other people have, then you may be cut out for a business as a window-washing entrepreneur. Though many people will think you're crazy for wanting to dangle from skyscrapers with only a system of pulleys and cables to protect you, the truth is that most prospective window washers, who admit to a fear of heights, quickly adjust to the altitude. Becuase the industry isn't typically touted as one of the hottest businesses for aspiring entrepreneurs to start, window washers are in demand. As a result, once word gets out that you're in business, you may soon have more work than you can handle.

The good news about becoming a window washer is that you can probably specialize in residential work, if you don't live near an urban area or are especially fearful of being higher than two stories off the ground. Many homeowners—whether they do it themselves or even know that they can hire somebody else to do it—would love to have the outside of their windows cleaned on a regular basis, but few put it on their priority list. You'll want to sign them up for automatic visits two or three times a year so you won't have to wait for them to call you when their windows get too dirty to see through.

Part II:
Entrepreneurship 101

Before you proceed to run headfirst into starting the kind of business in which you don't have to work hard anymore, it's a good idea to take some time to evaluate yourself, your financial situation, and the skills you'll need to run your business. Doing your homework at this stage will save you from making big and possibly costly mistakes down the road.

Assessing Your Personal Goals

First, you must determine what your overall personal goals are and how running a business fits in with them—and vice versa. Take some time to answer the following questions in detail:

- ▸ What are the three main reasons why you want to start your own business?
- ▸ How do you envision a typical day, running your business?
- ▸ How long do you plan to run the business?
- ▸ Do you view running your business as a part- or a full-time commitment?
- ▸ What are your personal goals, aside from being an entrepreneur? Do you plan to retire at a certain age, or move on to something else after running the business for 10 years?

Many entrepreneurs view their businesses as a means to a specific end: It provides a way they can go into partial or early retirement, or perhaps it's the only way they can finally move to a rural area and still be able to make a decent living. They can also start a business in the same field in which they've been working their butt off for *others* for years.

Other people dream of the self-sufficiency they'll be able to achieve by running their own business. Certainly people who want to give up long commutes to an unsatisfying job or who dream of spending more time with their families will begin to start a business for this reason.

You need it to provide income along with a healthy dose of satisfaction. You also need to have something in your life besides the business. That's why it's important to set goals for yourself that are totally separate from the business. Burnout is very common when you start a business in which you'll face constant deadlines. One way to prevent it is to plan your personal goals—that is, those that have absolutely nothing to do with the business—in advance. Whether your goal is to learn a foreign language or spend more time with your friends and family, in this business, it is both possible and very necessary.

Assessing Your Financial Goals

If you want to get rich, go buy a book by Charles Givens. If you want to have a decent income while you build equity and increase your revenues a bit each year, then keep reading.

To see if your financial goals jive with running your own business, ask yourself the following questions:

> ▸ What would you rather have after 10 years of hard work: A large sum of money in the bank or equity in a valuable business that would be relatively easy to sell?

> ▸ What's the least amount of money you could live on each month, provided that the mortgage, taxes, and utilities are paid for?

For most people who decide to start a business, initially, money is a secondary concern. Of course it takes money to get a business up and running no matter what kind of company you decide to start, but if you've picked up this book, it probably means that you're concerned about your lifestyle first and your income second. These priorities will help keep you motivated during the times when the money is slow.

Many people who would like to start their own business shy away from it for financial reasons. They can't see risking part of their hard-earned savings or paycheck on a venture that may or may not make any money for them. In most instances, starting a business is all about financial risk, at least in the beginning. The possible payoff is great and the financial success will come your way if you pursue an idea that has a definite market. But the bottom line is what kind of security you need to feel comfortable. There will undoubtedly be days when things will be touch and go in your business, especially during the first year. Therefore, if you feel safer with your money in a CD or savings account, then choose one of the businesses that require very little money to start, and start slow.

Assessing Your Tolerance for Risk

Many people who dream of starting their own business may love the idea and constantly fantasize about it. When it comes right down to it, most will never take the necessary steps because they're reluctant to leave the security of a regular job, health insurance, the familiarity of a particular lifestyle—you name it—even if they're unhappy in their current lives. A person who falls into this category has a low tolerance for risk of any kind.

On the other hand, if you can tolerate risk (even welcome it to some degree) and recognize that, even though everything necessary is done to operate and promote the business, there is still an element of risk that any one person is unable to control, such as economic downturns and fickle weather, then you are right for this business. Accepting this as a normal part of doing business, you can proceed accordingly.

What's your tolerance for risk? People who don't have a high tolerance for risky situations often see the world in black and white, with no room for gray areas. Sure, the prospect of quitting your job or cutting back to part-time and starting a business is frightening—even to people who like some excitement in their lives. There's no safety net. What makes you think you can pull this off? What if you fail? These are probably only a few of the concerns that are running through your head before you decide to start your business. However, men and women who are able to see these factors as challenges to meet and surpass and who like not knowing what the next week will bring should be able to deal well with the unpredictable nature of running their own business.

Sometimes, in order to get into the business, it's necessary to do without the things you treasure. Many people finance their business by selling family heirlooms, cars, even their homes, when there's no guarantee they'll be able to succeed. If you place great importance on your possessions and hate the idea of essentially gambling with them, you should think twice about spending a lot of money to start your own business, or else find some-one else to finance it.

Attitude Requirements

In my eyes, the ideal person to start a business is someone who's a cynical optimist, or, as some might say, an optimistic cynic. This is a person who has a positive attitude toward the world, but who also is not terribly surprised when things go wrong. When that happens, you spring into action and do whatever it takes to address the problem and get everything back to normal—until the next time.

As a entrepreneur, you'll be dealing with a variety of people and situations, as well as a business that, in essence, is operating 24 hours a day—at least in your mind. As a result, surprises will come up from time to time, especially in the beginning. As long as you maintain a positive attitude and remain alert to problems that need your immediate attention—while having patience for those issues that can wait—you'll be able to successfully start a business and maintain your equilibrium as well. And remember: At least once a week, you should take a few hours to get away from the business, especially if you work from a home office. This will help you maintain your positive attitude as well.

Perhaps the most important aspect of the attitude you'll need to start a business is firm fixation on your business and a strong belief in your subject. This, more than any other part of your personality, will give you what it takes when you're dealing with current and prospective customers, as well as those times when you need a heavy dose of motivation to pull you through any lulls you may experience.

Your Assets and Liabilities

Before you start working on the first issue of your business, it's a good idea to analyze your assets and liabilities—personal, financial, and those that involve your house, if you choose to work from home.

Starting any business is rough. Living in the same place where you work can also present a strain. Many people who run a home-based business find that one solution is to close the door to their office to take a break. Nevertheless, a home-based business will affect your entire family. How will you and your family cope with the adjustment? Good communication and developing a plan in advance to share some private downtime together each day is a definite asset and will help prioritize your goals about running a business.

As for money, experts always say you should budget at least twice as much as you think you need. By the way, the same philosophy also applies to the amount of time you'll need to get your business up and running. In terms of money, you'll need a financial cushion of several months' regular income to cover both personal and unexpected business expenses, at the very least, and financial experts usually recommend much more than this figure. There are always extra expenses that come up that you hadn't budgeted for, or an emergency will arise that requires an immediate infusion of cash, such as renting a booth at a trade show or a special deal on an ad in a trade publication. The important thing to know is that your liabilities can be addressed quickly if you have the assets—that is, the extra cash—to fix them as soon as possible.

Small Business Administration

The Small Business Administration (SBA)—which you help to pay for with your tax dollars—is a veritable gold mine of information, if you want to start your own business. There are three major divisions within the SBA that can assist you in the start-up phase of your business, as well as provide you with advice and assistance once your business is up and running.

One is the Small Business Development Center (SBDC), which counsels entrepreneurs in every conceivable type of business and at every level of development. The SBDC will set you up in private sessions with an entrepreneur who has experience running a business, or at least has hands-on experience in the communications industry. You can ask about any phase of running a business that you'd like, from marketing to locating suitable financing to how to keep your business going in tough times.

The SBA also runs the Small Business Institute (SBI) on a number of college campuses nationwide. Each SBI tends to specialize in a given field, from engineering to business management, but if you're looking for very specific information, contact the nearest SBI that has the program you want. The assistance at an SBI is largely provided by students in the program, but always under the watchful eye of a professor or administrator.

SCORE, or the Service Corps of Retired Executives, can be an exciting place for you to get information about your business. SCORE officers provide one-on-one counseling with retired business people who volunteer their time to help entrepreneurs, such as yourself, get the help they need. All the volunteer counselors have extensive experience in a particular field and are eager to share their insights. SCORE also offers a variety of seminars and workshops, on all aspects of business ownership, that aspiring entrepreneurs can also attend; you'll get specific advice about the nuts and bolts of running a business, in general, from bookkeeping to taxes. The Small Business Administration also offers a large variety of helpful booklets and brochures on all aspects of running a business.

To locate the SBA and its other programs, look in the phone book under "United States Government." Call the office nearest you for information about the programs and services they provide locally. To contact the SBA in Washington directly, write to them at:

> The Small Business Administration
> 409 Third Street S.W.
> Washington, D.C. 20416

To get in touch with the variety of services, visit the SBA online at *www.sba.gov*.

Organizations That Help Small Businesses

Once you start running your own business, you'll be in good company as you join millions of other Americans who are operating their own small businesses. Specific questions can pop up, and you'll undoubtedly want to network with other entrepreneurs, who aren't necessarily in the same field, to get your questions answered. There are a number of nationwide associations that provide small business owners with information, specific resources, discounts on business products and services, and the ability to work with other members.

The following is a list of a few nationwide organizations that have proven to be valuable to the entrepreneurs who join them:

National Association for the Self-Employed
PO Box 612067
Dallas, TX 75261
800-232-6273

www.nase.org

National Federation of Independent Business
53 Century Boulevard, Suite 250
Nashville, TN 37221
800-NFIB-NOW

www.nfibonline.com

American Woman's Economic Development Corporation
216 E. 45th Street, 10th Floor
New York, NY 10017
917-368-6100

www.awed.org

National Association of Women Business Owners
8405 Greensboro Drive, Suite 800
McLean, VA 22102
800-55-NAWBO

www.nawbo.org

National Minority Business Council
25 West 45th Street
New York, NY 10036
212-997-4753

www.nmbc.org

Planning Your Business

Planning is the key to the success of your business. If you set out without a plan, you're essentially setting out on a lengthy cross-country car trip without a map. You'll spend a good deal of time relying on the advice of other people for information on where to go and how to get there, instead of your own plans, dreams, and instincts.

This is why it's important that you take the time now to plan your business down to the smallest detail. It's the single most important thing you can do to ensure the success of your business, especially if you don't want to work hard anymore.

Planning to Succeed

Before starting a business, every entrepreneur *expects* to succeed. However, only a handful *plan* to succeed, and therein lies the difference.

Planning to succeed means you'll have to think about how you envision your business, as well as write a business plan. Though many businesses do succeed without developing these planning materials, you're more likely to succeed if you take the time to plot out every aspect of your business, from designing your logo to deciding how you'll answer the phone.

Getting the details down in writing will not only help to clarify your vision of your business, but it will also provide you with a blueprint to check every so often, to see that you're on target and on schedule. If you're not, you'll be able to backtrack to discover why you've been delayed or if your original plan was a bit too ambitious.

Writing Your Business Plan

It's important to have a business plan, even if you know exactly what you're going to do, where it will be located, and when you want to do it. Even if your goals are not that specific at this point, you probably have an idea of the type of business you'd like to start after skimming through the list provided in this book.

Writing a business plan will help you to map out a specific blueprint to follow, on your way to meeting your business goals. A business plan allows no question about even the smallest aspect of getting your business off the ground. After all, in the confusion and excitement, many things get overlooked. Getting it all down in writing provides you with a detailed itinerary. Because you'll write the plan yourself, you can tailor it to your own needs and tinker with it later, when unforeseen roadblocks begin to emerge.

With a business plan in hand, you'll be able to show the bank, your suppliers, and other potential business contacts exactly how you visualize your business, in language and figures they understand. But writing is a funny thing that reveals a lot as it unfolds. Not only will your business plan provide you with a broad picture of your business, in addition to allowing you to get all of the little details down in writing, but you'll also come up with other things, as you think, write, and plan aspects of your prospective business, that might not have occurred to you otherwise.

Having a business plan written before you do anything else for your business will put you way ahead of your competition, because most businesses do not take the time beforehand to plan out their strategies as carefully.

Although a business plan is vital to the successful start-up of a business, you shouldn't tuck it away in a drawer and forget about it. It is meant to be used and referred to as you progress in your business. Periodically checking the progress you're making against the goals you put forth in the plan allow you to see where changes need to be made, as well as whether you're keeping up with, or even surpassing, your original goals.

As I've mentioned, one of the top reasons businesses fail is a lack of planning. Writing a detailed business plan that is geared toward the type of business you want to start will allow you to see if your goals fit in with your budget, if you should wait until you've raised more money, or indeed, if this is the right business for you after all.

Anyone who reads your business plan will be able to get a clear picture of the type of business you want to start, as well as its projected financial health. Spend the time on it now—if you run into trouble later on and don't have a business plan to refer back to, it just might be too late.

A business plan can be only a few pages long or a massive 100-page document that maps out every single detail involved in running your business. Though it takes more time, it's best to err on the side of quantity when writing a business plan. The more you know about your business before you open the doors on the first day, the better prepared you will be for the surprises that may come your way.

A business plan should have four main parts. The first part includes a cover sheet, your statement of purpose for the business, and a table of contents. Then comes the meat of the business plan: Section One describes the business—what you provide, your target markets, your location, competition, and the personnel you expect to hire. Section Two concerns financial information about the business—income and cash flow projections and, if you're buying a business from another owner, the financial history of the business as they ran it. The last portion of your business plan should consist of supporting documents that back up the information you're providing in the other sections—a resume of your employment history, your credit report, letters of reference, and any other items you believe will help the reader to better grasp what you are striving to do with your business.

For a library of sample business plans, visit *www.businessplans.org*. The bible of writing a business plan is widely considered to be *The Business Planning Guide* (Kaplan Professional Company, 2002), by David H. Bangs.

Writing Your Marketing Plan

Though you do cover marketing to some extent in your business plan, developing and writing a separate, detailed marketing plan will serve the same clarifying purpose to your marketing efforts as to the development and daily operations of your business.

As is the case with a business plan, when it comes to marketing, without a concrete plan to follow, it's easy to let marketing fall to the bottom of your daily and weekly to-do lists—or even forget about it entirely. Also like your business plan, in your marketing plan you'll define your purpose as well as the target audience you wish to reach with the various tools in your marketing arsenal. You'll be able to design a marketing budget that is reasonable and aggressive at the same time, pick your preferred media, and explain the methods you'll use to evaluate their results. This will help you to alter your marketing plan for the following year.

Marketing is usually considered to be an afterthought, something that is to be performed grudgingly when an advertising deadline looms or after you attend a trade association meeting and decide that your brochure and other promotional materials look painfully out of date compared to everyone else's.

You can make marketing your business tolerable and even sometimes enjoyable by mapping out a specific plan each year that won't let you off the hook so easily. If you say that, in March, it's time to send out your new brochure, and your budget for that month allows for it, you'll do it.

The primary mistake that entrepreneurs make in their marketing is to rely too heavily on advertising, both when they're first starting out and later on. I'm not saying that advertising doesn't work, because in some cases it can pull quite well. However, it often turns out to be the most expensive way to reach customers, especially when your 1-inch display ad is only one of hundreds in a particular publication.

Advertising is easy because you tell the sales rep what you want to say, you write out a check, go over the proof, and receive a copy of the magazine. In other words, somebody else does all the work. But it doesn't necessarily produce the results you desire, which is an increase in the number of customers.

Spending your time and money on promotion—whether it's sending out a press kit or renting a booth at a trade show—is harder, and doesn't provide you with a guaranteed entity, that is, an ad in print. What it will do is provide you with increased exposure among your targeted customers; they'll notice you simply because you'll stand out. After all, the majority of businesses take the easy way out, spending the bulk of their annual marketing budget on advertising and perhaps printing another 1,000 copies of their brochure with what's left over.

Developing a marketing plan will help you to take a long-range view to spread your efforts among a variety of opportunities. It will also help you to anticipate certain events that only happen once a year. Like your business plan, a marketing plan is also meant to be tinkered with. For example, if a specific advertising opportunity comes up in September, or you hear about an idea that has worked wonders for another similar business nearby and you want to try it, you look at November and December and see you don't have much scheduled. Even though your monthly marketing budget allows for $100 and you need $175 for this new idea, you can combine the money from those two months and pay for the project.

There are four different aspects to a marketing plan. They are:

1. The amount of time you will spend, on both a daily and weekly basis.
2. The type of marketing you plan to do, whether concentrating on magazine publicity, newspaper ads, or revamping your brochure and business cards.
3. The amount of money you want to budget for each month and for the total year.
4. The person who's going to carry out each task. For some businesses, only one person will be responsible for writing copy, working with a graphic artist, and doing interviews with the press. Even for the smallest businesses, some entrepreneurs decide to spread out the responsibilities to ensure they get done, and to provide a fresh eye.

Market Planning Assessment

To draw up your annual marketing plan, you'll have to answer a lot of questions. You'll need to be as complete as possible, however, to design the best marketing plan for your business. Answering the questions in the five sections that follow will help you to identify the issues that you'll need to address.

Time

- How much time do you spend each week on marketing your business?
- Provide a breakdown of how many hours you'll spend each week on publicity, advertising, direct mail, and other areas. Do you feel this is enough time? Do you think you're using your time effectively?
- Would you like to spend more or less time? What would you spend it on, or where would you cut back?

> ▸ When do you project your busiest seasons to be? How far in advance should you begin planning for the various media and projects that you want to do?

> ▸ After your first year in business, look back over the year. Which months were slow in terms of business? Which were busy?

Media

> ▸ In which media would you like to focus more of your marketing efforts?

> ▸ What type of marketing brings you the most customers?

> ▸ What kind of customer would you like to see more of? How would you reach them?

Budget

> ▸ What percentage of total sales does your marketing budget comprise? How could you increase—or decrease—that amount? What other categories could you take money from?

> ▸ Do you have an annual or a monthly marketing budget now?

> ▸ Would you like to invest more money in one or more categories? Which ones? Why?

Execution

> ▸ Name the person or people currently responsible for marketing. Is there anyone else to whom you feel comfortable assigning additional duties?

> ▸ Are there additional tasks you could assign to a staff member—tasks that you don't like to do or don't have enough time for?

Customers

▸ If you're running a national business, in which area of the country do most of your customers live? Are they concentrated in one industry, or is their profession not a consideration?

▸ What type of customer would you like to attract more of? How can you target them? Why would they be attracted to your business?

One good source for sample marketing plans is located at *www.morebusiness.com*. A good book is *Marketing Plans That Work* (Butterworth-Heinemann, 2000), by Malcolm McDonald and Warren Keegan.

Should You Buy a Business or Start From Scratch?

If you decide to start your business from scratch, you will need to do more work from the beginning than if you buy an existing business. The advantage of starting your own business is that it usually costs less. It will also bear your personal stamp from the outset. Buying a business means that you'll have to work within a framework that may not fit your own. If you choose to tinker with it, you may lose customers. Another disadvantage to starting your own business is that it may take awhile before the money starts to come in on a regular basis. You will also need to work hard on developing and building your reputation.

The main disadvantage to starting a business from scratch is that you won't have income from it until you start *running* it, which usually takes longer than your initial estimates. In fact, while you do pay more at the outset for an existing business, it can start producing revenue for you from the day you move in. As you assume ownership, you also control the bank account and any orders or contracts that come in after the transfer of ownership. You should weigh the pros and cons against your own temperament before you proceed.

If you buy an existing business, most of the business technicalities have already been set up for you, though you will have to have everything transferred to your name. You also have the advantage of having a track record to which you can compare your own efforts, though you still need to write a business and marketing plan.

Buying an established business means that you have the advantage of starting out with a good reputation, and a ready-made list of customers. Sometimes, buying an existing business will actually cost less than starting from scratch, if you factor in the reputation of the business, the customer list, computer equipment, and other amenities that are included in the purchase price. And if you figure that your labor is worth something, even though you probably won't be paying yourself a salary for quite some time, buying a business outright may turn out to be a veritable bargain.

Your Business and the Law

With any business, there are certain legal restrictions that you have to meet. The first thing you need to do is register your business with the state. There will be a fee for this, and the purpose is to make sure that no other business is currently operating with the same name. If there is, you will have to find another name for your business. Registration will also alert the state to expect tax revenue from your business. If you don't file a return with the state, they'll know where to find you.

When you register with the state, you should also ask about other regulations you have to meet in order to operate your kind of business in the state where you live. Most of the time, they will refer you to your town, which is responsible for determining zoning and other business regulations and will collect the fees from any permits for renovations that you need to make.

If you neglect any one of the steps necessary to open and operate a business in your town, the government authorities have the power to shut down your business or do whatever is necessary to bring your business into compliance. The time to find out all of this is before you open your doors, so it pays to do your homework first.

You'll also need to determine the form of business you'll run: a sole proprietorship, a partnership, or a corporation. Each has its advantages and disadvantages, and entrepreneurs have very specific reasons for picking one over the others.

Sole Proprietorship

A sole proprietorship is the form of business that most single-owner businesses pick. It's easy to start; all you have to do is register with the state and you're in business. You make all the decisions yourself, and except for zoning concerns regarding running your business from your home, you're pretty much free from having to follow complex laws regarding the operation of your business. You alone are responsible for the success or failure of your business, and any profits that your business earns are reported as income in your name.

However, because there are few restrictions on a sole proprietorship when you run into legal or financial trouble, dealing with it falls on your shoulders. For many entrepreneurs, liability insurance that's tied in with your business or homeowners policy will often be enough to handle a "reasonable" lawsuit and settlement. The remote chances of being hit with a lawsuit and the relative ease of operating this form of business ownership make a sole proprietorship the preferred method of business organization for most entrepreneurs.

However, if your business should fail, you will be responsible for all outstanding debts incurred during the course of doing business. If you don't pay them, or if you declare bankruptcy, it will be reflected on your personal credit record.

Partnership

A partnership is actually two sole proprietorships combined. This means that while the strengths are doubled, so are the inherent weaknesses.

The most common instance where a entrepreneur decides to create a partnership is choosing to enter the business with a friend or business partner. Married couples also sometimes decide to form a partnership when they start a business together. Though a partnership usually means that twice as much energy and money are available than in a sole proprietorship, you should consider it very carefully before you proceed. The best partnerships work when the partners have differing but complementary talents—and they leave the other partner alone to do what they do best. For instance, at one business, one partner may have a strong background in day-to-day business operations, while the other loves nothing more than to deal directly with customers. As long as each trusts the other to concentrate on their own department, and to interfere only when problems arise, the partnership will probably do well.

Partnerships usually run into trouble when the partners have similar skills and/or different ideas about the right way to run a business. For example, when both partners want to concentrate on working with customers instead of dealing with the behind-the-scenes tasks, you can be sure there will be problems right from the start.

As with a sole proprietorship, if somebody decides to sue the business, both partners are personally liable. And if the business fails, leaving outstanding debts, you are both responsible. You should also realize that if one partner disappears after a business fails, the other must pay all debts. Be aware of this, because it does happen from time to time.

Corporation

A corporation is best defined as an inanimate object, a business organization that has its own guidelines, aside from those of the business, which include financial and legal restrictions. It's more difficult, expensive, and time-consuming to form and operate your business as a corporation, but it also absolves your formal personal responsibility in case the business sours or in the rare case that someone decides to sue.

One advantage that corporations have over partnerships or sole proprietorships is that this form of business can raise money by selling shares in the business; the only recourse the other two have is to borrow money from a bank or from friends.

A corporation is, by nature, more unwieldy than the other two because of its responsibility to its shareholders, who are really part-owners. The Internal Revenue Service taxes corporations on a different scale than sole proprietorships and partnerships, and there are even more rules and regulations a corporation must follow on both the state and federal level. There are also certain restrictions on the types of operations a corporation can perform. Some expansion and growth issues, for example, require the approval of stockholders before a project can proceed.

Some entrepreneurs automatically opt for incorporation to protect their personal assets in the case of a lawsuit, and this is prudent. However, a business that will benefit most from incorporation is when there are more than two owners controlling the future of the business. With multiple partners deciding the fate of the business, issues of ownership and decision-making become more complex, so it becomes easier to rely on a board of directors and group of stockholders, especially because they've invested their money and trust in the business.

Do You Need an Attorney?

Whether or not you choose to use the services of an attorney to help you set up your business before you open your doors depends on how you view the legal profession in addition to how detail-oriented you are. Some entrepreneurs swear by their lawyers and consult with them about every decision that needs to be made. Others swear *at* them, and will never use an attorney for anything in their business or personal lives.

The happy medium is somewhere in between. If you're planning to incorporate your business, you'll probably need to use a lawyer, although more people are learning how to incorporate on their own. It has been my experience that the vast majority use a lawyer to help facilitate the process.

If, however, you're buying an established business, you will undoubtedly have to hire an attorney to negotiate the terms of the contract. Aside from this, you will probably be able to do most of the tasks involved in starting your business without a lawyer.

Do You Need an Accountant?

If you're unsure about the type of business organization that suits you best—sole proprietorship, partnership, or corporation—it's a good idea to consult with an accountant to help you decide. An accountant will analyze your current financial situation and help you determine what you want to gain from running your business in terms of revenue—equity or income—and advise you about how to best achieve your goals.

An accountant can also analyze the books and financial records of a business that you're thinking about buying. It's a good idea to find an accountant who has some experience keeping the books for small companies.

You may want to ask other entrepreneurs in your area for the names of some accountants they'd recommend, then call up each accountant and interview them before you settle on one.

An accountant can also help you set up a realistic budget and a schedule of projected revenue. If this is the first time you've run a business of your own, a professional accountant can help you become familiar with different accounting methods, the tax rates based on projected revenue, and the tax codes of your state. An accountant can also recommend methods of bookkeeping that will make their job that much easier when tax season rolls around.

Licenses and Permits

Before you open for business, you must check with the local, county, and state business authorities to find out about the various kinds of licenses and permits you'll need in order to be licensed, if any. Also, if you're running a business out of your home, you should check with your local town ordinances to see if there are any restrictions on home-based businesses. All of these vary from town to town and from state to state, so I'm not going to go into detail about them here.

I will, however, describe the purpose of the licenses and permits you will be required to get. Bear in mind, however, the stringency of these requirements will also vary as well. States and regions with more highly regulated governments tend to be pickier about what you can and cannot do with your business, as well as the fees they charge you for the privilege of making enough money to pay taxes.

Even though you may resent all the legalese and paperwork, it's important to meet all of the requirements—but no one says you can't complain every step of the way. You'll need a sales tax certificate from the state to collect tax. A health inspector may need to ascertain whether your septic and water systems can accommodate the increased demands that employees and visitors will place on them.

Even if your home and facilities successfully meet all of the above regulations, if your home is not in an area that is zoned for business use, you may be out of luck and will need to run your business from an office in an area that's especially zoned for commercial use. However, it's your town government that determines zoning and is also responsible for making exceptions for small businesses that are located outside of commercial zones. Your business will provide a tax base for your town and help bring more money to local businesses that you will frequent, but because you will have a commercial enterprise operating in a residential area, you will probably have to apply for a zoning variance.

The rules get creative, though. Some towns will allow you to operate your business at home as long as you don't hang out a sign. Others will require that you, as owner, live in the house and not in a separate building. You may also have to expand your driveway and parking area to accommodate an increased number of cars.

Far more interesting laws governing small businesses in your area undoubtedly exist. That's why it's important to check all of the requirements *before* you do anything.

Managing Your Money

Once you get your business up and running on a regular schedule, it's important to keep track of your expenses and revenue sources. There are as many ways to keep records as there are entrepreneurs. Some rely on a standard spreadsheet computer program. Some stuff receipts in shoe boxes and dump them out at the end of the year, leaving a large task for their accountant to handle.

Most entrepreneurs use a variety of methods to help them keep track of their money, both revenue and expenses. The basic record will probably be your checkbook. There are a number of business checking accounts that come with built-in ledgers where you can record your expenses under different expense categories at the same time you write a check. Separating these expenses in advance makes it easy at the end of the year to determine how much you've spent in each category, and if you need to cut back.

Some entrepreneurs prefer to keep their financial records on computer. Software now exists to enable you to keep track of your expenses, categorize them, add them up in a flash, and even write checks that are printed by your computer printer.

To keep track of your revenue, you should keep a record of each transaction. There are a number of specialized software programs that can help you keep track of your revenue and expenses, plus provide other features, such as word processing and database tracking.

Whatever method you choose, make sure that it's easy to use and that you check in at least once a week. Going longer than that will make keeping track of your money a chore and something you're likely to put off, which will make it more likely that you'll make mistakes. If you're like most entrepreneurs, you'll discover that it will be difficult to find an uninterrupted block of time anywhere in your week unless it's in the wee hours of the morning.

In the unlikely case of a tax audit somewhere down the road, it will undoubtedly help boost your case if you can show the auditor receipts that provide answers to all questions. Keeping good records will also help facilitate figuring out the deductions you'll be able to take.

At the very least, you should get a ledger book to organize your records. Some business checking accounts now offer a shortcut in the form of a built-in ledger that allows you to break down the checks you write into different expense categories thus eliminating the need for a separate ledger.

Also, some of the companies that you'll do business with are making it easier for their customers to keep track of their money. Credit and charge card companies now offer a breakdown of charges in different categories on their monthly statement. Some of the suppliers with which you maintain an account will also provide this service. And if they don't already do this, ask; they might start.

Accounting Basics

Once you start your business, you need to keep track of revenue coming in and expenses going out. It's a good idea to set up an accounting system that works best for you and your business.

There are two kinds of accounting you can use to track revenue and expenses. One is cash accounting and it involves simple bookkeeping where income is recorded when it is received, and expenses are recorded when bills go out, even if the expense was incurred in a different month. With cash accounting, you will record the revenue in the month where it may not have necessarily occurred. This may give you an inaccurate picture of your business cycles if you rely on revenue alone to show the health of your business. Cash accounting, however, is a very simple way to keep your books, and many entrepreneurs prefer it for its simplicity. They tend to be running a small one-person business that is not yet pulling in a significant amount of money. As a result, they don't need a precise picture of their month-to-month revenue and expenses.

Accrual accounting is more painstaking in its execution, but it gives a more accurate view of revenue and expenses, and of your monthly financial situation. Even though payment may be received or credited the following month, they are recorded in that month's ledgers, and not when they were actually paid. This includes expenses paid on a net 30 system (that is, customer payments are due within 30 days of the invoice, after which interest is charged) because they occurred in the previous month.

When drawing up your accounting system, think carefully about the method and categories that will work best for your business.

Employees and Taxes

Some entrepreneurs prefer to keep their operations small, one-person businesses, specifically so they'll be able to handle all the jobs themselves without having to hire outside help. Hiring and managing employees adds a whole new dimension to your business and has both its good and bad points. For one, it means more paperwork because you'll have to pay state, federal, and perhaps local payroll taxes, in addition to Social Security, workers' compensation, and insurance (if you decide to offer it). On the other hand, having someone around to help out with the grunt work means you'll have more time to focus on aspects of running and building your business, such as marketing and exploring new products to sell to your growing customer base.

Unfortunately, a common complaint of business owners everywhere today is that it's hard to find good help. After all, no paid employee is going to regard your business and customers in the same meticulous and painstaking light that you will. So you'll probably have to lower your standards of quality and attention and plan to spend some time making up for the lack.

With the rise in unlawful sexual harassment suits filed as the result of being fired, entrepreneurs have been further discouraged from hiring help, even though they may want to. However, many entrepreneurs advise that if you find an employee who is the exception to the rule, hold onto that person as tightly as you can by increasing his or her pay, offering bonuses, and letting this person know how much you appreciate him or her with added responsibilities and the occasional day off with pay.

When hiring employees, there are certain things you have to do. If you're hiring a person to work for you regularly—writing, answering the phone, or stuffing envelopes—they will be considered your employee and you will have to deduct taxes from their paycheck, to file with the government either quarterly or once a year, depending on your tax setup.

Some businesses get around the process of withholding and payroll taxes by preferring to hire an employee as an independent contractor. This way, the contractor files a self-employment tax, which saves you a lot of paperwork. This works for such seasonal and periodic workers as gardeners and musicians, but it will send up red flags with the Internal Revenue Service if you try to hire a part-time office assistant in this way. If you do hire an independent contractor, and pay them more than $600 over the course of a year, you must file a 1099 form, on their behalf, which reports their income.

No matter how you decide to "hire" an employee, make sure that you always communicate with them clearly and directly and immediately when there's a problem or complaint. And let them know when you think they did a job well.

Understanding Taxes

When you first set up your new business and discover how much time, energy, and paperwork you devote to taxes, you might wonder when you'll find the time to actually run your business. Between payroll taxes and your own income and other personal taxes, it can all seem pretty self-defeating at this point. Why go into business if most of your revenue will go toward taxes?

First of all, take a deep breath. It only seems overwhelming now as you're learning about your different responsibilities. Once you get used to it, recording and paying taxes—as well as figuring out your deductions—will turn out to consume just a small part of your bookkeeping and office time.

You will also be required to keep track of your revenue and expenses and to pay a tax to the Internal Revenue Service on any profit your business earns. The amount of tax you pay will depend on the type of business you're running—a sole proprietorship, partnership, or corporation. The tax structures for each differ.

Of course, because start-up costs for some businesses are significant during the first couple of years that you're in business, your expenses may exceed your income, so you won't have to pay tax. The Internal Revenue Service allows that there will be years when you'll earn no profit on paper, even though it assumes you are in business to earn a profit. As a result, many businesses claim a wealth of deductions to avoid showing a profit, and therefore, paying tax. That's why current tax law says that you must show a profit at least three years out of five to prove that you are running a viable business. If you show a loss three or more years out of the five, it will alert the Internal Revenue Service and set you up for the possibility of an audit. This is why some entrepreneurs, even though they may lose money on paper in a given year, may decide to "forget" about some deductions just to avoid arousing the suspicions of the Internal Revenue Service. Keep in mind that the deductions claimed by home businesses will occasionally come under more scrutiny from the Internal Revenue Service due to the home-office deduction taken.

As for payroll taxes, contact your state employment bureau about the exact deductions you should make for each employee and the federal tax bureau for information about income tax, Social Security, and other payroll taxes.

Profits and Losses

One important way to gauge how your business is doing is to calculate a profit and loss statement. Even though money may be coming in regularly through revenue, it may be possible that you are actually losing money because your expenses exceed your income.

Keeping accurate records will help make preparing a profit and loss statement much easier; all you have to do is plug in the numbers. There are two kinds of profit and loss statements you can keep: one that projects your estimated profits and losses, and another that keeps track on a weekly or monthly basis to help you see how well your business is doing. You can also compare the two. If your projections are either 20 percent higher or lower than your actual figures, based on slow and peak times, this method will enable you to adjust your projected profit and loss statements as you go along.

To figure out your profit and loss statement for your business, you must first calculate the revenues you expect to generate each week, month, and/ or year. Your business may not be a huge money-maker for you in the beginning, but once you make a list of all of your operating costs, using either actual figures or estimates, add up all of your expenses for the year, it'll be easy to operate at a loss. Include everything: postage, printing costs, phone bills, rent and utilities, business loans, and anything that you paid out in order to operate your business.

Don't forget about depreciation. Ask your accountant for advice on this, but chances are that you'll be able to deduct the amount that is deemed to depreciate on your house, office equipment, and other big-ticket items this year. This is not strictly an expense, but will serve to help lower your profit, which will then lower your tax bill.

Don't forget about the interest you pay on any loans connected with the business. And remember that the type of business you run—sole proprietorship, partnership, or corporation—will also affect your profit and loss statement.

After deducting all of your expenses from your revenue, you'll be left with a pretax profit or loss. There's one more step, though. Now deduct all of the taxes you pay in connection with your business—except payroll taxes, which are figured into your payroll expenses—and you will come up with your actual net profit or loss, which probably seems a long way from your initial gross revenue figure.

Though you'll always have certain fixed expenses, there are a variety of ways you can adjust your profit and loss statement. Cutting your expenses, discounting or raising your prices, and increasing your marketing efforts are just a few. Over time, you will be able to see what attracts new customers and what keeps old customers coming back. You'll also see that running a business is a constant experiment; your profit and loss statement is merely a constant reminder of how well your experiment is doing.

Developing Your Credit

If you're in business for any length of time, you're going to need credit in one form or another. Most of the time, it will be from suppliers who deal with you on a regular basis and who don't pick up cash or checks with each delivery they make. (Writing out invoices and collecting payments are the jobs of the accounting department, not the delivery people. If an entrepreneur asks the company to make an exception, payments and invoices often get lost.)

But most suppliers and other companies won't offer you credit unless you've done business with them before. It's the age-old catch-22: How can you develop your credit if no one will give you any in the first place?

Fortunately, there are ways around this. Many companies will open a credit line for you based on your personal credit record. They'll usually start you out small, and then increase your credit line as your history with them grows. Needless to say, you'll help your credit line if you always pay promptly, even before the due date, and by acting promptly whenever they or you have questions about your account.

With other suppliers, you'll need to prove yourself in the beginning—and your personal credit, no matter how stellar, will have nothing to do with it. These companies will make you pay cash or by check before they deliver the goods, and only after a certain period of time will they begin to extend you credit, and only a little at a time.

Once you begin to establish a credit record for your up-and-running business, you'll undoubtedly be solicited by charge card companies that invite you to open a business account with a high credit limit and low monthly payments. Though having a business credit account helps in many instances, such as renting a car or buying airline tickets, try not to use them too much. Cards are almost universally accepted (even the Internal Revenue Service takes MasterCard and Visa now) and, because it's easier to slap down the plastic than to apply for a basic account with a supplier, you might be tempted to run up huge bills with their inherently high interest charges. This is a high price to pay for apparent convenience. Instead, use them sparingly, appreciate them for what they are—an extremely expensive way to borrow money—and be as judicious with their use and payment as you are with your other creditors. After all, they can help develop your credit rating too.

And although banks are a lot pickier now about lending money even to people with unblemished credit ratings, you might apply for a line of credit at your bank, if you don't have one already. Learning to rely on it only in emergency financial situations, then paying back the money immediately will help your business get through the tough times.

Working With Suppliers

As I've already said, one part of working with suppliers is building up credit and establishing a working relationship. However, getting the best price may be the most important thing to you. Other entrepreneurs might be attracted by a printer's twice-weekly pickup and dropoff schedule, while still others might favor a supplier because of the particular brands the company carries.

Most suppliers will bend over backwards to get your business, though you may find that you'll have to jump through a few hoops at first—to get a credit account set up in your initial dealings with the company for instance.

There are many ways to find the suppliers who will work with you and who you'll feel most comfortable working with. You should know if one supplier doesn't give you the terms you'd like, there are others who will. Don't sign on with one right away—take the time to shop around for the best price, the quality you want, and the working relationship you feel comfortable with. Whether you prefer to deal by mail, have the items delivered to your door, or pick them up yourself, it's easy to find the best supplier for your business, from promotional items to paper for your laser printer.

Borrowing Money

The issue of borrowing money in these credit-weary days is apt to be a sticky one among entrepreneurs who may have taken out a loan to finance their businesses. "I'm in enough debt already," you may say. "Why would I want to borrow any more?"

Sometimes your cash flow won't keep up with your expenses. Even if you (and/or a partner) hold down a steady job, trust me when I say there will be times when even that won't be enough. Operating a regular business with all of the expenses that continue steadily from month to month will eat up huge amounts of cash. During those times, it may be necessary to borrow money.

If you have a rich relative or a sizable trust fund, you can skip over this section. But if you're like most of us, you'll need to rely on a conventional financing source. Because you already know to anticipate these cycles, especially in a business that's usually known for its peaks and valleys throughout the year, you should take steps now to line up an available source of credit that you can draw upon immediately.

I know of many examples where entrepreneurs have drawn on their credit cards to initially finance their business, and then have gone back to them when things got slow. At anywhere from a 12- to 21-percent annual rate of interest, this is definitely an expensive way to borrow money. Even if you fully intend to pay it back before interest has a chance to accumulate, there will be times when you are only able to make the minimum payment.

Some entrepreneurs form partnerships for the sole reason of having a silent partner, with deep pockets, who's looking for a good rate of return on his or her money. But if you prefer to have a partner for other reasons or to go it alone and you don't want to have to rely on your credit cards, there is another option, and that is to open a line of credit at your bank.

If you don't want to go this route—or get turned down—there is the old-fashioned way: Save for a rainy day. When business is booming and revenue is strong, set aside a certain percentage—some say 20 percent of every order that comes in—and sock it away in an interest-bearing savings account. Don't invest it in a place where you don't have instant access to your funds; even though the interest rate may be less, you'll probably pay more by paying a penalty for early withdrawal from an IRA, mutual fund, or other investment. A money market fund is best; the interest rates tend to be a little higher than a passbook savings account, and you have immediate access to your money.

How to Raise Additional Capital

Because the revenue from your business can be sporadic at times, especially in the beginning, many entrepreneurs turn to other sources of income. Most other businesses are concerned with raising additional capital to initially finance their business, Even though their cash flow may be cyclical, the ups and downs in some businesses are probably not as extreme as the cash flow in others. To raise additional capital to finance a business, some people turn to parents or relatives, while many rely on the proceeds from the sale of their primary house and move, in order to start their business in an area where they can live mortgage-free and plow all the revenue from the business back into the business. For others, with mortgages and no regular income, the best way to raise the additional capital needed to keep the business afloat is to increase the number of products and services you offer, which you can sell to both existing customers and prospective customers alike.

You have to be creative to stay in business these days, no matter what your venture is. The advantage of other services that you offer is that many of them will result in additional business for your business, thus bringing your efforts full-circle.

How to Give Credit to Customers

The primary way that most entrepreneurs extend credit to their customers is by accepting the several major types of credit cards that are popularly used today. MasterCard, Visa, American Express, and Discover are accepted by many entrepreneurs. The credit card companies will charge a fee to set you up with their service, and then you'll pay the credit card company a percentage of every transaction made by a customer, usually two to five percent. Your account is typically credited within one to three days after you enter the transactions into the system, and there are certain restrictions each company places on its members, depending on the amount your business will gross each year, among other factors. It is relatively simple to apply for privileges that will allow you to accept credit cards from your patrons, although you may have to jump through a few hoops with financial statements, tax returns, checking account statements, and other proof that you run a trustworthy business and you won't go out of business six months down the road.

The reasons? It may seem unfair, but credit card companies like to grant merchant status to retail businesses with an actual storefront because, in this business, the staff is handling actual credit cards, and customers see the total amount on the slip they are signing. Mail-order businesses are immediately suspect because they're not dealing with the physical card.

My advice is to keep looking and applying until you are accepted, because your revenues will instantly increase once you start to accept credit cards. If you decide against it, you may never know how profitable you may have become. Indeed, whether or not you accept credit cards may make the difference between whether or not your business succeeds or not—unfortunate, but true. If someone sends a credit card number along with his order, and you write back to tell him you're not set up to accept plastic yet and request a check, you may never hear from him again.

However, some entrepreneurs decide not to accept credit cards from their customers. Either their volume is too low to justify paying the commissions, or else the credit company places too many restrictions on them. Some have also said that the companies tend to have a patronizing attitude toward smaller companies—such as entrepreneurs—because they simply don't provide the commission revenue that larger businesses do.

Whatever way you decide to extend credit to customers, it's important that you do offer it in some form. We have a love-hate relationship with it as a society. But because we do rely on it, you should arrange for it before you start running your business, if at all possible.

Improving Cash Flow

Cash flow is defined as the pattern of movement of cash in and out of a business: revenue and expenses. Even though operating your business will mean that the cash flow will be highly erratic at times, you can, to some extent, predict when your cash flow will slow down and when it will be high. This will help you to see during which months you should stockpile some of your excess cash in order to provide you with cash flow and income in the downtimes.

If you apply for a loan with a bank or other financial company after your business is up and running, you'll have to provide an analysis of your cash flow. If you're just starting out, you may be required to provide the loan officer with a projected cash flow statement.

Cash flow includes all actual monies coming into and going out of the business, including cash, checks, and income from credit cards. Depreciation of your computer and other office equipment does not factor into your cash flow analysis.

The first step toward improving your cash flow is to increase your business year-round. But the effects from this aren't always immediate, and there are thing you can do to even out your cash flow a little more. Tying in with your projections, you might want to conduct special promotions designed to pull in more sales during those times of the year when your cash flow needs boosting the most. For instance, you should plan to mail special offers to your customers in your slow months. Or you can send out direct mail packages offering your ancillary items to past and present customers.

Another way to even out your expenses and, therefore, to improve your cash flow is to ask your utility companies to average out your payments so that you basically pay the same amount each month year-round. If you stash away 20 percent of your gross revenue during the busy times, as suggested earlier, you'll have money to draw on during the slow months.

The Growth of Your Business

Growing a business today can be a challenge. Though everything you will do as an entrepreneur will, in some way, influence how your business grows, most of the time your thoughts will not be on growth, but on putting out all of the little fires that will pop up each day. If you have any time or energy left at the end of the day to think about growth, it may be along the lines of how to slow it down so that you'll have at least 15 minutes each day to call your own. Seriously, growth—or the lack of it—is an issue that every entrepreneur has to face at one time or another. This section will show you how to deal with the variety of ways that growth will manifest itself in the operation of your business. And if you've gotten this far in your determination to run your own business, handling growth will probably turn out to be the least of your troubles.

Many entrepreneurs feel that of all the business problems to have, those that involve issues of growth are among the easiest to handle. It's not always so. Although growth, as a rule, means increased revenue and business, it also means more work and expenses, as well as more headaches to deal with.

Some businesses will grow at a slow steady rate of 8 to 10 percent a year. Others will explode after a glowing article in a large-circulation magazine or major newspaper appears. Which is better? While some prefer slow growth as a way to allow them to learn about the business and grow into it, others say that rapid and/or sudden growth provides them with a real education on what running a business is all about and provides a needed boost to the business when the owner might have otherwise been hesitant about forging ahead. This kick in the pants is sometimes exactly what an entrepreneur needs.

Growth *can* be managed and controlled to some extent. How you do it and whether you do, however, is up to you. Some of the choice is manifested in the ability to limit the number of customers through the prices you charge and limiting the amount of marketing you do over the course of a year. Indeed, there are a handful of businesses that pride themselves on their exclusivity and do indeed limit the number of customers they take on. This is the ideal way to run things from the beginning if you don't want to work too hard.

One issue you'll face with a growing business is whether or not to hire employees. If you already have help, you'll have to decide whether you should increase their hours to full-time or hire more workers.

Your business is your baby, and if you're used to doing it all yourself you may find it hard to delegate some of the responsibility to someone else, even if it means more free time for you. Most entrepreneurs have difficulty letting go at first, but with time and as you begin to see the high level of the ability of the people you do hire, you will trust in them more, which will leave you with time to turn to other problems in the business that need to be addressed.

Another by-product of growth is what to do with the extra money. Some entrepreneurs use it to pay off some of their personal debts, but the Internal Revenue Service will automatically count these monies as personal income. It's best to do this over time, though some people feel that the savings you'll make in not paying debt interest will more than offset the increased tax you'll have to pay.

Some entrepreneurs use the extra money to pay off home mortgages. Though it may feel good to own your own house free and clear, the interest you'll be able to deduct from your mortgage payment each month for your home business office can come in handy in keeping your taxes down, especially because your business will likely show a larger profit with increased income.

One method that many entrepreneurs use to invest the money and keep their profits and therefore their taxes down at the same time is to upgrade office equipment and purchase a new phone system or the latest desktop system each year. This will not only cut your taxes, but you'll be able to streamline your operation and also handle more volume, which will increase your revenue—and your *profits*—so that next year you'll have to do the same thing all over again. Granted, though, it's a nice problem to have. Of course, as I've already explained, you will have to show a profit three out of five years if you're operating as a sole proprietorship or partnership. But if you've been growing steadily, this will not be a problem.

Managing Employees for Greatest Efficiency

The art of management once prescribed that a boss or manager should rule with an iron fist. Both employer and employee knew who was in charge. Employees went along with this facade, but more often than not, they managed to get away with things whenever they could and did only what was expected of them, never anything more.

The opposite philosophy was that of the sensitive manager. He soft-pedaled harsh news, coddled his employees, and was always ready to lavishly praise even the tiniest accomplishment. Again, employees went along with it, but felt they were never fully trusted or appreciated for their own talents and efforts. As before, quality and morale suffered.

The ideal management style for a small business is to let employees feel as though they are responsible for the business's success or failure. They will treat it as though it were their own—an attitude which only comes with certain responsibilities. This style is perfect for entrepreneurs who need to delegate. Working closely also allows staffers to quickly develop a personal relationship with the boss. This type of management may run counter to what many people think being a boss ought to be, but in the end, you'll find that your employees will be happier and more productive, and will also stay with you longer if you learn to manage them in this way.

It's not easy to do this, however. People who feel they have to control their employees in order to get them to work may run into problems with executing this altered style of management. However, once you see that your employees will treat your business almost as well as you do, it won't take long for you to become a proponent of this management style and actually begin to adopt it in other areas of your life.

Here's how to do it. Say you need to hire an employee to work 20 hours a week at your business, helping out wherever you happen to need it. First, determine the tasks he is best at, and which of those he would feel comfortable being left alone to execute.

Train him by going through the various tasks with which this employee will need to become familiar, from answering the phone to taking phone orders to printing out a press release on the computer. Have him watch you do it a few times, and then let your new employee do it alone. Assure your employee that he can approach you with any questions, no matter how trivial they may seem. Encourage open communication at all times. Your end of the deal is to remain open to queries and always respond in a patient manner.

Then, once it appears he has one task down pat, give him another one. For instance, if he is comfortable with taking phone orders, you might let him take the next logical step, entering the information into the computer or sending out handwritten welcome letters to new customers.

If your employee makes any mistakes, call them to his attention immediately, and then patiently and without judgment, explain the way to do it that's best for the business and *why*. Make sure that it's not just because the new employee is doing the tasks a bit differently from how you would do it. In fact, for maximum efficiency, try not to get too caught up with how things get done, rather, that they *do* get done. If you insist that your employees follow certain steps in order to reach the final solution, you'll find that you'll be trying to squeeze a lot of round pegs into square holes. The outcome may turn out the same, but the morale may not, and your efficiency will, as a result, probably drop.

Then, as your employees' responsibilities grow, increase their pay based on performance and give regular bonuses and days off with pay. The idea is for employees to feel personally responsible for the satisfaction of every customer so that your time is freed up to work on other projects without worrying about the business.

The secret to successfully managing employees is to show them what to do, trust that they'll do it, and then leave them alone. Though many employees will be taken aback by this unique approach, and some will find it to be too alien for their tastes, the great majority will meet the challenge and help to build your business, while cultivating a personal relationship with you.

What works best is to show your employee what the final result should look like, and then go off and do your own thing. As long as the basic quality of the job isn't compromised, it helps to learn to look the other way. Some entrepreneurs are perfectionists, however, and they think that no one else knows how to do things the right way. Unfortunately, this kind of manager will find it hard to keep employees and may be burned out by the end of their first year in the business.

Though you're still calling the shots, compromise and acceptance is the name of the game when it comes to managing employees and maintaining the steady growth of your business.

Secrets of Success

In my opinion, along with many other entrepreneurs nationwide, the number-one key to success in any industry is marketing. In this instance, I use the term quite loosely; not only does marketing encompass all of the traditional channels, such as advertising and publicity, but it also includes your own personal public relations campaign, or how you interact with your customers.

During every minute that a customer is exposed to your business—on the phone, through the mail, or in person—you should be marketing your business in a positive light. I'm not talking about the hard sell. After all, they're already customers. The secret of success is to get them to continue doing business with you and to tell their friends about the value of doing business with you. This means being constantly aware of whether or not your business is continuing to meet their needs, and to figure out—or merely ask—if there's anything more you can do to improve on what you're already doing. At the same time, however, you should expect that some customers won't welcome this degree of personal interaction with you. In these cases, you'll have to let your business do your marketing for you.

But remember: Your marketing job never ends, and that goes for both kinds—the marketing to prospective customers as well as every contact you have with current customers. If you cease to market, you will soon fade from your customers' memories because it's obvious you didn't care enough about their satisfaction, and one of your competitors will undoubtedly be waiting in the wings to take your place. After all, with thousands of messages bombarding your customer base each day, you need to stand out to succeed. But that doesn't mean a constant hard sell, either.

It may seem a bit redundant to add this, but your happiness and satisfaction are also keys to success in running your business, especially if you don't want to work hard anymore.

Reality Check

Despite the fact that you may have started your business because you don't want to work hard anymore, every entrepreneur has experienced a time when they've been so busy, or so involved with their business, that they have learned to tune out the world as a whole and not venture beyond the office except to go grocery shopping. Some even get someone else to perform these outside tasks for them.

When you start your business, you'll probably be operating your business from your home. If you're used to commuting to an office every day, you should be prepared for a shock, because you'll have to motivate yourself, and there will be no one else around to do it. In addition, the constant interruptions and lack of personal time can quickly begin to skew your perspective on life and the world. Even if you have regular contact with lots of people over the phone, if you don't venture out at least a few times a week, it's entirely possible that your attitude will begin to change.

That's why it's imperative to get away from the business for a full afternoon or evening at least once a week. Or take one day a week off. Do something that has nothing to do with the business. Do something for yourself for an extended period of time or you'll need to refer to the following section a little sooner than necessary.

When to Quit

Burnout and oversaturation with their industries are the major reasons why entrepreneurs decide to sell or close down their businesses. It's so very easy to become caught up in running your business to the point where you have no desire to do anything else. This is precisely why many entrepreneurs are working more and more, and why some choose not to hire employees, even if they need the extra help desperately and lose sight of why they decided to start a business in the first place.

Another reason why entrepreneurs decide to get out of their businesses is closely tied in with reason number one: Running a successful business—or an unsuccessful one, for that matter—is a lot more difficult than it appears on the surface. They underestimate the amount of work it tkaes and overestimate the money that the business will generate—especially the money they think will be available for their own personal use.

Because of these skewed expectations, sometimes people tend to quit their business long before the time they plan to leave otherwise. Five years is frequently cited as the typical amount of time an entrepreneur will be in business before he or she gets the feeling it's time to move on to something else.

Of course, entrepreneurs who still love what they're doing may feel one or all of these symptoms at one time or another. But the secret to knowing when to quit is when you feel like moving on and believe the disadvantages of running a business outweigh the advantages.

You may decide to opt out of the business, and in fact, may sell your business to someone who's new to the field. ("Remember when we were that enthusiastic?" you may say.) But, as is often the case, many entrepreneurs who leave the business jump right back in a few years later.

So take heed: Once you start, you may not be able to stop. After all, running a business, if you don't want to work hard anymore, will get in your blood, and it will be hard to get it out.

Index

O

Ohmae, Kenichi, 88
old house restoration, 127-128
organizations that help small
    businesses, 184-185
Organizers, National Association for
    Professional, 144
organizing, professional, 144-145
outplacement consulting, 128-129

P

pack and ship service, 130
*Painting Contractor: Start and Run a
    Money-Making Business*, 131
painting, 131-132
partnerships, 194-195
Peake, Jaquelyn, 20
permits, licenses and, 197-198
personal chef, 133-134
personal financial planning, 135-136
personal fitness training, 137-138
personal shopping service, 138-139
Pet Age, 140
*Pet Sitting for Profit: A Complete
    Manual for Professional Success*, 141
pet specialty manufacturing, 140-141
pet-sitter service, 141-142
plan
    business, 186-188
    marketing, 188-190
planning,
    children's party, 34-35
    personal financial, 135-136
    reunion, 153-154
    wedding, 172-173
pooper scooper business, 143-144
processing, medical claims, 117-118
Professional Association of Custom
    Clothiers, 52
Professional Association of
    Innkeepers, 26
professional organizing, 144-145
profits and losses, 202-203
property consulting, intellectual, 107-108

Property Law Association, American
    Intellectual, 107
public relations consulting, 146-147
Public Relations Society of America,
    The, 146
publishing consulting, electronic, 72-73
publishing,
    desktop, 58-59
    e-zine, 79-80

Q

quit, when to, 214-215

R

Ramsey, Dan, 131
Reader's Digest, 125
Recruiters Online Network, 73
recruiting, employee, 73-74
recycling pick-up, 148-149
relocation consulting, 149-150
Relocation Council, Employee, 149
*Renovating and Restyling Older
    Homes*, 127
repair, computer, 44
restaurateur, 151-152
restoration, old house, 127-128
Retailer's Bakery Association, 25
reunion planning, 153-154
Rightlook.com, 23
risk, assessing tolerance for, 181-182

S

Sachs, Patty, 34
sales, classic car, 38-39
*Sales: Building Lifetime Skills for
    Success*, 154
sales rep service, 154-155
Sawyer, Deborah C., 106
*Sawyer's Survival Guide for
    Information Brokers*, 106
Schultz, Kate, 79
SCORE, 76
Scrap, 148
secretarial service, 156-157
seminar leader, 157-158

About the Author

LISA ROGAK is the author of more than 25 books on cooking, travel, health, business, and pets. She lives on the edge of a cliff in Grafton, New Hampshire, with 14 cats.